"By privileging a Mediterranean social script and its cultural codes as the most appropriate way to clarify Phoebe's role in the first-century Jesus groups, Campbell reminds the reader of the cultural distance separating the first century and the twenty-first century believer."

— *J. Dorcas Gordon*
Knox College, Toronto

"Masterfully executing traditional and social scientific exegetical analysis of just two biblical verses (Rom 16:1-2), Campbell draws a fresh picture of Phoebe as she has never been understood before except perhaps by her contemporaries. Situating Phoebe solidly within her Middle Eastern cultural context clarifies and enhances this plausibly authentic image of a very important woman among the earliest Jesus Groups. Campbell's lucid presentation of complex interdisciplinary research and her engaging writing style recommend this book to a wide audience."

— *John J. Pilch*
Georgetown University
Washington, DC

"Using the lens of a woman who is mentioned only once in the New Testament, Joan Campbell's *Phoebe* introduces the reader to key aspects of ancient Mediterranean history, geography, and culture, and provides a marvellously clear exposition of such diverse topics as ancient naming conventions, letter delivery, the culture of Corinth and its port, Kenchreai, the use of fictive family language in early Christianity, and the culture of patronage and clientism. A lucid introduction to the culture in which the Jesus movement was born and flourished."

— *John S. Kloppenborg*
Professor and Chair
Department and Centre for the Study of Religion
University of Toronto

D0912335

"Joan Campbell takes her readers on a fascinating tour of Phoebe's socio-historical world, squeezing rich insights out of a meager biblical account in Romans 16:1-2. In an elegantly written and engaging style, Campbell introduces Phoebe through the geographical setting of the port city of Kenchreai, through the ancient social system of patronage/clientage, through the political role of emissary, and through the familial role of sister. Phoebe, who has been relegated over the centuries to an obscure and insignificant role within the Pauline communities by means of inaccurate and androcentric translations of Romans 16:1-2, is reinstated in this work as Paul's powerful and invaluable partner in the spread of the Gospel to the gentiles."

—*Lee A. Johnson*
Methodist Theological School in Ohio

Paul's Social Network: Brothers and Sisters in Faith
Bruce J. Malina, Series Editor

Phoebe

Patron and Emissary

Joan Cecelia Campbell

A Michael Glazier Book

LITURGICAL PRESS
Collegeville, Minnesota

www.litpress.org

A Michael Glazier Book published by Liturgical Press

Cover design by Ann Blattner. *Saint Paul*, fresco fragment, Roma, 13th century.

Maps on pages 37 and 43 reproduced by permission from Jerome Murphy-O'Connor, OP, *St. Paul's Corinth: Texts and Archaeology* (Collegeville, MN: Liturgical Press, 2002), 7, 18. © 1983, 2002 Jerome Murphy-O'Connor, OP.

1   2   3   4   5   6   7   8   9

Library of Congress Cataloging-in-Publication Data

Campbell, Joan Cecelia, 1956–
    Phoebe : patron and emissary / Joan Cecelia Campbell.
        p. cm. — (Paul's social network, brothers and sisters in faith)
    "A Michael Glazier book".
    Includes bibliographical references and indexes.
    ISBN 978-0-8146-5281-7 (pbk.)
    1. Bible. N.T. Romans XVI, 1-2—Criticism, interpretation, etc.
    2. Phoebe (Biblical figure)   3. Paul, the Apostle, Saint—Friends and associates.   4. Kekhriai (Greece)—Antiquities.   5. Women—Social conditions.   6. Women in the Bible.   I. Title.

BS2665.52.C36 2009
227'.1067—dc22   2009014142

For my family
My siblings
Michael, Celeste, Patrick, Hugh, and James

And in loving memory of our parents
Martha Reta Hennessey (1921–2007)
Cyril Francis Campbell (1918–2008)

CONTENTS

PREFACE

Human beings are embedded in a set of social relations. A social network is one way of conceiving that set of social relations in terms of a number of persons connected to one another by varying degrees of relatedness. In the early Jesus group documents featuring Paul and coworkers, it takes little effort to envision the apostle's collection of friends and friends of friends that is the Pauline network.

This set of brief books consists of a description of some of the significant persons who constituted the Pauline network. For Christians of the Western tradition, these persons are significant ancestors in faith. While each of them is worth knowing by themselves, it is largely because of their standing within that web of social relations woven about and around Paul that they are of lasting interest. Through this series we hope to come to know those persons in ways befitting their first-century Mediterranean culture.

Bruce J. Malina
Creighton University
Series Editor

ACKNOWLEDGMENTS

This book could not have been written without the support of many people. I would like to thank Dr. Bruce Malina for inviting me to contribute a volume to this series and Dr. John Pilch for providing me with helpful bibliographical leads. Special thanks to Dr. Joseph Lee Rife, who kindly provided me with a copy of an unpublished paper, "Religion and Society at Roman Kenchreai." For the opportunity to devote myself to writing, I am indebted to Atlantic School of Theology, whose sabbatical policy enabled me to bring this book to completion. The research was also assisted by a grant from Pine Hill Divinity Hall (United Church of Canada) that provides short-term employment for student research assistants at the school. My thanks to Maya Bevan for a job very well done! Members of the library staff at Atlantic School of Theology, especially Ian Fraser, document delivery, and access services, were very generous with their time and assistance. Finally, I owe an enormous debt of gratitude to the religious community of which I am privileged to be a member, the Congregation of Saint Martha of Prince Edward Island, my sisters in faith, whose encouragement and prayers have sustained my studies and research these many years. To all of you, I am enormously grateful.

INTRODUCTION

Who Is Phoebe?

Says Phoebe Snow
About to go
Upon a trip to Buffalo
"My gown stays white
From morn till night
Upon the Road of Anthracite." (Advertising Jingle, DL&W)

On time the trip
Ends without slip
And Phoebe
Sadly takes her grip
Loth to alight
Bows left to right
"Goodbye dear Road
Of Anthracite." (Advertising Jingle, DL&W)[1]

The Delaware, Lackawanna, and Western Railroad (DL&W) connected Pennsylvania's Lackawanna Valley, which was rich in anthracite coal, to New York City, Buffalo, and Oswego, New York. Around the turn of the twentieth century, Earnest Elmo Calkins created an advertising icon for the DL&W.[2] His icon was a young New York socialite and a frequent train passenger whom he christened Phoebe Snow. Miss Snow often traveled to Buffalo, New York, and her garb, white from head to toe, was chosen to symbolize the cleanliness of the coal-run trains. In no time, Phoebe was enjoying enormous popularity throughout the country. Women, in particular, were captivated by her image. The fact that she traveled alone challenged the social norms, and she became the symbol of a new kind of woman whose independence was welcomed by many. Women, however, were not her only admirers. Advertising jingles, such as the two cited above, became so popular that they were even sung on Broadway. Moreover, actresses dressed as Phoebe Snow appeared at special events and civic celebrations. It was only when the government prohibited the use of anthracite coal in steam locomotives during World War I that Phoebe was retired. Gone but not forgotten, she reemerged in white military attire during World War II to play up the railroad's contributions to the war effort. In 1949, the DL&W launched a passenger run from Hoboken, New Jersey, to Buffalo, New York. The signature train, the Phoebe Snow, operated until 1966. During these years, the image of Phoebe Snow, the socialite, continued to stir the imaginations of patrons, particularly women for whom she once more modeled a new cultural image. By 1966, Miss Snow had enjoyed almost seventy years of notoriety, and during those decades her image left its mark on American culture.

The legacy of Phoebe Snow has intrigued not a few historians. How, they ask, did she manage to rise to the status of cultural icon? The answer to this question has proven to be no simple matter. The records of Earnest Calkins, who died in 1964, have assisted this reconstruction but provide only sketchy information about how she acquired such enormous popularity. Phoebe's path to success continues to elude historians. While this is unfortunate, it should come to us as no surprise. Written records cannot say everything. Even detailed accounts are finite and unable to provide us with exhaustive information about the subject matter. Memories soon fade, and with the passing of time and the disappearance of those most familiar with the issue, historical reconstruction becomes increasingly challenging.

Although little more than one hundred years separate us from the origins of Phoebe Snow, a reconstruction of her path to success is a daunting task. Imagine, then, trying to find a window into the life of an individual who lived approximately two thousand years ago and who hailed from a culture vastly different from our own. Moreover, consider the difficulty when the only written record that mentions this character consists of two biblical verses. As difficult as it might seem, the task of this book is to find glimpses into the life of such a character, oddly enough, another Phoebe, Phoebe of Kenchreai,[3] an associate of St. Paul. While she shares little more than her first name with the glamorous Phoebe Snow, her status and rise to fame are equally enigmatic.

How, you might ask, will we achieve our goal when we have but two New Testament verses (Rom 16:1-2) that speak directly of our Phoebe? The answer to this question lies in our choice of interpretive approach. Biblical scholars espouse a range of different methods in their study of texts, depending on the purpose driving their study. The method chosen for a particular task is closely related to the types of questions that the scholar entertains. While this is not the place for a detailed review of several methods of biblical exegesis, brief mention of three will illustrate the point.

One well-established method of investigating biblical texts is known as the historical-critical method. When scholars employ this method, they pose questions about things such as the influence that writers (copyists) had on the formation of biblical texts, the literary relationships among the canonical gospels, or issues concerning the groups for whom these documents were written.

Sometimes, however, scholars prefer to investigate documents as timeless literary texts, just as they are for us, without concern for the historical context in which they were written. Using modern literary criticism, these scholars ponder largely nineteenth-century issues such as plot, characterization, irony, or symbolism and how these elements function within the text.

A third type, and the one used by this book, employs a historical method known as the social-science method of biblical studies, a type of anthropological history. Basically, this approach attempts to understand the cultural world of the people who populate the pages of the Bible and to apply this information to our reading of biblical documents. Fundamental to this approach is the understanding that particular words do not mean the same thing in every culture. Further, the meaning of the words in any text, including biblical texts, is derived from the social system out of which those texts come.[4] Therefore, in order to understand the words that we read in biblical texts such as Paul's letter to the Romans, we must understand the social system within which Paul and his audience communicated. Although his words about Phoebe are few, they are a rich resource for studying the cultural world in which she lived.

Phoebe's World

In many ways, Phoebe's world is foreign to us. For one thing, education was limited almost exclusively to elites, and writing materials were both scarce and expensive. There were a few educated scribes, but the vast majority of people could neither read nor write. In fact, some historians argue that only about 5 percent of the people could read and even fewer could write. For most people, then, hearing, speaking, and observing were the primary vehicles by which information was learned and passed on.

In this oral-dominated context, storytelling was a popular means of communicating information. As tales were told and as epic ballads were sung or recited, performers adapted them to make them relevant to the lived experience of their audiences. Over the centuries, this pattern of reshaping stories and songs perdured in areas of the world such as the Middle East. Even today, no two singers of traditional Middle Eastern songs produce identical performances of the same selection.[5] Each time a musician plays or sings a particular song, he or she introduces variations and additions, depending on the mood of the gathering. Anthropologist Raphael Patai observes that Middle Eastern storytellers also treat the tradition as flexible. While the basic story is preserved, each performance involves the creation of a new variation on the original theme. This is not how contemporary North Americans normally experience the transmission of songs, stories, or scriptural texts. In general, songwriters record and copyright their lyrics and sing the same lyrics each time they perform the piece. Furthermore, storytelling is more dependent on books than it is in traditional Mediterranean societies, which exhibit a higher degree of orality.

In the first century, the primary vehicle by which Israel's sacred writings (Old Testament) were transmitted was the spoken word. Most people heard biblical stories only when someone else read them aloud or performed them in a context devoid of the written text.[6] While today we hear biblical passages read on occasion, such as during worship services, our norm is to function as *readers* rather than *hearers* of the Bible. For first-century Christ-believers, however, word of mouth was the dominant means by which virtually all information, including the Scriptures, was received. The same was true of Paul's letters. The vast majority of people *heard* them; they did not *read* them. Since this context placed so much emphasis on conversation as the primary vehicle of information communication, the transmission of information was highly interpersonal and relational.[7] Therefore, when Paul's letter was read to Jesus groups in Rome, conversation about what they heard played a pivotal role both in how the letter was received in that particular group and in how members of that group conveyed its contents to others.

Another important aspect of Phoebe's cultural context is that she lived in a preindustrial, agrarian world that differed vastly from much of twenty-first-century North America. The word "agrarian" derives from the Greek word *agros,* which means "field" or "land." Hence, agrarian societies are agricultural as opposed to industrial, hunter-gatherer, or fishing societies.[8]

Agrarian farmers use the plow rather than the hoe and depend on large animals such as oxen, horses, and donkeys.

In most regions of contemporary North America, the farming scene is clearly not agrarian. On the contrary, much of today's food production is accomplished with the aid of complex machinery rather than animals. Therefore, when we read the New Testament, we must remember that we have been removed from its cultural context by two millennia, as well as from a way of life bereft of the tremendous cultural changes brought about by the Industrial Revolution. Nevertheless, despite the enormous social distance between us and New Testament writers, it is possible, with the help of social-scientific methods of biblical studies, to reconstruct, at least partially, the outlook and way of life of biblical personages like Paul and Phoebe. The reason for this is that the culture of traditional Middle Eastern societies has changed very slowly, so slowly that the lives of traditional groups such as village-dwelling peasants and transient Bedouin[9] are still comparable to those of biblical peoples. In fact, while changes have certainly occurred, the cultural patterns of traditional Mediterranean societies are much closer to biblical cultural patterns than are those of any other surviving groups.[10] Patai says the following:

> Folk life in the nineteenth- and twentieth-century Middle East is essentially comparable to the life of the ancient Hebrews as reflected in the Bible. No student of culture would, of course, assume that life in the Middle East has remained unchanged in the three and a half millennia which passed since the days of Abraham. Changes have occurred, as they must, in every century and in every generation. But in the Middle East, possibly more than any other world area, changes have been slow. The way of life and even the physical appearance of a village in Palestine or in Syria of the twentieth century are consequently very similar to what they were in the days of David. The same holds good for the nomads of the Syrian Desert who greatly resemble the nomads among whom was the ancestral family group of

the Hebrews. All folk society exhibits the trait of conservatism beneath superficial and insignificant change. Middle Eastern folk society is characterized to a remarkable degree by the persistence of the basic underlying pattern. Thus it is completely legitimate, from a methodological point of view, to seek a fuller understanding of what the Biblical characters did and said and thought through observing how the folk societies in "Bible lands" behave and speak and think thirty to thirty-five centuries later.[11]

We cannot stress enough the enormous social distance between us and the people we read about in the Bible. When we project our twenty-first-century North American values and perceptions onto what we read there, we produce interpretations that are anachronistic and ethnocentric, common pitfalls. Imagine yourself, a twenty-first-century reader, among a group of first-century Christ-believers. All of you are listening as someone reads Paul's letter to the Romans. The first few words describing Phoebe ("I commend to you our sister Phoebe") include a concept used by people of every culture from antiquity to the present—her name (Rom 16:1). Will your understanding of how names function in society mirror that of the remainder of the group? If not, wherein lies the difference?

Names

Many cultural symbols that we use on a daily basis were also used by biblical peoples but did not necessarily convey the same kinds of information. Names are no exception. My baptismal name is Joan and my family name is Campbell. I am usually introduced as Joan Campbell. While people often ask me who my parents are or what profession I practice, this information never becomes incorporated into my name. First-century Mediterranean societies, however, were different in this regard. Jesus was known by labels such as "Jesus of Nazareth, the son of Joseph" (John 1:45), the *tektōn* (a Greek word referring to one who worked with wood or stone), or "the son of Mary and brother of James and Joses and Judas and Simon" (Mark 6:3). Similarly, John was known as "the Baptist" (Matt 3:1), or more appropriately, "the Dipper." Mary, a disciple of Jesus, was designated "Magdalene" (Luke 8:2), thereby identifying her with the village of Magdala from whence she came. The point is that in first-century Mediterranean societies, names contained information such as one's geographical origins, names of family members such as one's father, or one's occupation. These labels communicated a great deal of information to others, in fact, all that they needed to know about one's social standing.

In the Bible, women are sometimes identified by their trade or place of origin. Lydia, for example, is a dealer in purple goods from the town of Thyatira (Acts 16:14). Women's names also reflect information about their families, particularly the identity of their husbands. In the gospels, we read of "Mary the wife of Clopas" (John 19:25); "Herodias," who was Herod's brother "Philip's wife" (Mark 6:17); and "Joanna, the wife of Chuza, Herod's steward" (Luke 8:3). In many cases, a wife's first name is not mentioned. Matthew's genealogy, for example, mentions the "wife of Uriah" (Matt 1:6). Bathsheba was a well-known figure in Israelite history (2 Sam 11:3; 12:24; 1 Kgs 1:11, 15-16, 28, 31; 2:13, 18-19). Perhaps Matthew thought it unnecessary to include her name because his addressees knew it well. Another example can be found in Luke's gospel where Jesus makes a cursory reference to "Lot's wife" (Luke 17:32). Here we have a situation where the woman's name is not recorded in the Septuagint (the Greek translation of Israel's Scriptures with which Luke was familiar) and may have been omitted by Luke because he did not know it. In any case, first names are often excluded in biblical references because it is one's family connections and geographical origins that are most significant.

It was also the case that women were identified through their sons (quite common among Palestinians). The mother *of the sons of Zebedee* requests that Jesus broker places of honor for her sons in his kingdom (Matt 20:20). She is also designated in this way when she, Mary Magdalene, and Mary, the mother *of James and Joseph* (note again how a mother is identified through her sons) witness the crucifixion and death of Jesus (Matt 27:55-56). In the Fourth Gospel, Jesus' mother is never called Mary. She is always referred to as "the mother of Jesus" (John 2:1, 3) or "his mother" (John 2:12; 19:25-26). Since the author of John appears acquainted with the parents of Jesus (John 6:42), it is unlikely that he did not know that Jesus' mother was called Mary. Why, then, would he consistently identify her through her son Jesus rather than use her first name?

Married women acquired honor by bearing sons. Even today, in regions of the world such as the Middle East, North Africa, and South Asia, there is a definite preference for sons over daughters, a phenomenon notable in the cultural world of Phoebe as well. An Egyptian papyrus, dating from the first century BC, contains the following instructions for a woman to expose her baby if it is a female:

> Hilarion to Alis his sister, heartiest greetings, and to my dear Berous and Apollonarion. Know that we are still even now in Alexandria. Do not worry if when all the others return I remain in Alexandria. I beg and beseech of you to take care of the little child, and as soon as we receive wages I will send them to you. If you bear offspring, if it is a male, let it live; if it is a female, expose it. You told Aphrodisias, 'Do not forget me.' How can I forget you? I beg you therefore not to worry. The 29th year of Caesar, Pauni 23.[12]

Boys were preferred because it was through the male line that the family name and its life would continue. Married women were considered subordinate in their husband's households until they bore one or more sons.[13] The birth of each boy increased the social status and power of a married woman within the household. Since bearing sons increased a mother's honor, it was common for others to refer to her as the "mother of X." This being the case, the Fourth Evangelist's use of the appellation "the mother of Jesus" may reflect the honor codes of the day. To say that she is the mother of Jesus signals the fact that she has a son and underscores the honor that goes with motherhood. Furthermore, she is the mother of *Jesus*. In view of the Fourth Evangelist's high Christology, one can be certain that the title "the mother of Jesus" heaps significant honor upon her.

No such kinship label is attached to Phoebe in Romans 16:1-2, however. She is simply Phoebe, a Greek name (*Phoibe*) that means "bright," "radiant," or "pure." There is no mention of father, husband, or sons. Paul does, however, label her as "our sister," a *diakonos*, and *prostatis*. Moreover, he provides a geographical reference—the town of Kenchreai. As indicated, these topics will be taken up in later chapters.

Paul's Letter to the Romans

At this point, it is necessary to say a few words about Paul's letter to the Romans, especially the final chapter that houses our reference to Phoebe. The letter to the Romans is unlike most of Paul's other authentic letters.[14] With the exception of Philemon, his authentic letters are addressed to Jesus groups that have grown out of his proclamation of the gospel of the God of Israel—but this is not the case with his Roman addressees. In fact, Paul says that he has often tried to visit them, but because of his work for God, he has been unable to do so (Rom 1:13; 15:17-22). In his letter, he comments that at last, he hopes his plan to visit them will be realized (1:10). Clearly, it was not Paul who originally brought the gospel to them. Why, then, does he write to them?

For one thing, Paul wants to announce his intended visit to Rome during which he hopes that they will exchange spiritual gifts and encourage one another (Rom 1:11-12). For another, Paul wants to garner support for his upcoming trip to Spain: "This is the reason why I have so often been hindered from coming to you. But now, since I no longer have any room for work in these regions, and since I have longed for many years to come to you, I hope to see you in passing when I go to Spain, and to be sped on my journey there by you, once I have enjoyed your company for a little" (Rom 15:22-24). The verb of seeing that Paul uses (*theaomai*) means to visit a person with friendly or positive intent. In other words, he wants to get acquainted with Christ-believers in Rome in order to establish a relationship of trust with them. Mention of Paul being sped on his journey implies that he desires their assistance in some way. The verb is *propempō* and means to send someone on with the intention of helping that individual. Paul is not simply planning a friendly visit: his time with them will have a purpose. In short, he needs their assistance if his Spanish mission is to be successful.

Robert Jewett explains that substantial numbers of Judeans did not live in Spain until at least the third century AD.[15] Therefore, Paul, who, according to Luke (Acts 9:20; 13:14-16; 14:1; 17:1-30), usually commenced his preaching in synagogues, would not have possessed his usual springboard for operations in Spain. Moreover, he would have faced linguistic challenges. Very few residents of Spain spoke Greek; the majority spoke native dialects or Latin, and translators would have been required. In this instance, Roman Jesus groups would have been invaluable to Paul because they would have been able to assist him in securing the necessary resources to get started in Spain.

If Paul were to garner their support, it would have been necessary for him to do some important groundwork. According to Philip Esler, a major reason why Paul wrote the letter to the Romans was to address ethnic tension and conflict among Judean and Hellenistic members of the Jesus groups in Rome.[16] Many of us are accustomed to using the terms "Jew" and "Greek" rather than "Judean" and "Hellenistic." But from a cultural point of view, "Jew" and "Greek" are inappropriate labels for first-century Mediterranean people.[17] "Judean" is preferable to "Jew" because members of the house of Israel referred to themselves as "Judeans" whether or not they lived within the geographical confines of the territorial region called Judea or in the Diaspora. Non-Judean peoples also referred to members of the house of Israel as "Judeans" because they associated them with Jerusalem and its magnificent temple in Judea. What about "Greeks"? In the first-century Mediterranean region, neither a nation by the name of "Greece" nor a group of nationals known as "Greeks" existed.[18] What we call Greece today was known in the first century as Macedonia (northern Greece) and Achaia (southern Greece). The word *Hellēn* (Greek) was an indicator of one's status; it referred to anyone who was "civilized," that is, to anyone who spoke Greek and adopted Hellenic values. Therefore, "Hellenists" is a more accurate designation for first-century Greek-speaking people.

Roman Jesus groups consisted of Hellenistic and Judean Christ-believers. The question of whether the Mosaic Law was necessary for them would have naturally arisen in groups comprised of both law-observant Judean Christ-followers and Hellenistic Judeans who had acquired "Greek" customs and values and who had never been adherents of the Mosaic law. On the one side, law observance was highly valued. On the other side, Hellenistic identity was given pride of place. Tensions were mounting between the two, particularly because the Hellenists disdained those who observed certain aspects of the Mosaic law, such as the food laws.[19] As we see in the letter, division among them is a huge problem for Paul, who needs their support (Rom 15:22-33). To get it, he must establish his leadership credentials and convince them that Judeans and Hellenists share a common identity in Christ. By bringing them together under the one banner of Christ, Paul hopes to ensure their cooperation with his Spanish mission. At the very least, his success could mean financial aid and translation services that would ensure smooth communication with the Spanish population.

It has often been thought that Phoebe was the bearer of Paul's letter to Roman Jesus groups[20] and that it was she who read it to them and responded to their questions. It has even been proposed that she had agreed to act as the patron of Paul's Spanish mission.[21] While these images of Phoebe are very attractive, their validity is integrally tied to an issue that is still debated in Pauline studies—whether chapter 16 of Paul's letter to the Romans was originally destined for Jesus groups in Rome.

The Destination of Romans 16

The majority of interpreters maintain that Paul wrote his letter to the Romans from Corinth[22] in approximately AD 56–58. Ancient Corinth,[23] inhabited as early as 5000 BC, was a Hellenistic city-state located on the Isthmus of Corinth, the narrow stretch of land joining the Peloponnesus to the mainland of Greece. Its location provided Corinth with great importance in Paul's day, as Corinth controlled the four-mile-wide isthmus, the only land route into the Peloponnesus. When Paul first visited ancient Corinth (AD 51 or 52), Gallio, the brother of Seneca, was proconsul (Acts 18:12). According to Luke, Paul resided in Corinth for a year and a half (Acts 18:11). While there is little reason to doubt that the first fifteen chapters of Romans were written from Corinth to Christ-believers in Rome, over the years, a number of scholars have challenged the conclusion that chapter 16 was destined for Rome. Since chapter 16 houses our reference to Phoebe, it is necessary that we both acknowledge and take a stand on this issue. Before we do, however, it is important to realize that regardless of the destination of chapter 16, Phoebe was an associate of Paul. According to Luke, Paul had sailed from Kenchreai to Ephesus (Acts 18:18-19). Given the proximity of Kenchreai and Corinth, Paul likely visited Kenchreai on several occasions and was well acquainted with Phoebe and the Jesus group in that town.

There is no scholarly consensus on the form of Paul's original letter to the Romans. While extant manuscripts include all sixteen chapters, there is external evidence that suggests that the letter may not have always existed in this form. An important biblical manuscript, the Chester Beatty Papyrus II (P^{46}) is an important textual witness in this debate. P^{46} is the oldest extant manuscript of Romans, dating to approximately AD 200.[24] While the letter of Romans that we know today concludes with a doxology in 16:25-27, that same doxology occurs between Romans 15:33 and 16:1 in P^{46}, thereby introducing the possibility that 16:1-23 was not part of the original letter to the Romans.[25] In fact, while the majority of today's scholars believe that 16:1-23 was always part of Paul's letter to the Romans, some are convinced that it was part of a letter of recommendation written by Paul for Phoebe that was destined for Ephesus but was appended to Romans at a later date by someone other than Paul. In the scholarly literature today, one finds arguments for and against the inclusion of chapter 16 in Paul's letter to the Romans. Some of the reasons offered by scholars to support Ephesus as the preferred destination for chapter 16:1-23 are listed below.[26]

First, the lengthy list of personal greetings (Rom 16:3-16) seems to suggest that Paul was well acquainted with several individuals in these Jesus groups. Since Paul had never visited Jesus groups in Rome (15:22), it seems unlikely that he would be able to greet so many Christ-believers there by name (16:3-15). We know from Luke, however, that some of these people were connected with Ephesus. For example, Paul met Prisca and Aquila in Corinth and worked with them for a while (Acts 18:1-3). Later, they went to Kenchreai and then on to Ephesus, where he left them (Acts 18:18-19). If one is to believe that the addressees of chapter 16 were in Rome and not in Ephesus, one must imagine that a large number of Paul's associates in the east had moved to Rome before Paul wrote Romans, something that not all scholars are ready to accept, since it seems that Prisca and Aquila were still in Ephesus when 2 Timothy was written (2 Tim 4:19).

Second, Paul's dear friend Epaenetus is said to be the first Christ-believer in Asia (Rom 16:5). Since Asia was a Roman province and its capital was Ephesus, such a comment is odd if chapter 16 were destined for a center in Europe, such as Rome.

Third, the content of Romans 16:1-23 seems abrupt following 15:33. Moreover, the warning against those who are creating dissensions and difficulties (16:17-20) is unusual if written by Paul to Jesus groups in Rome that he has never met; nowhere else in the letter does Paul attack his opponents with such rigor.

Fourth, early patristic authors do not quote from chapters 15 or 16. Advocates for a Roman destination of 16:1-23 refute these arguments. As of yet, no consensus has been reached on this matter.

There is another reason to conclude that Romans 16:1-23 was not destined for Jesus groups in Rome. More specifically, these verses may be a letter of recommendation for Phoebe, making special mention of her in 16:1-2. Paul was familiar with how letters of recommendation functioned. Recall his sarcastic words to the Corinthians about the apparent need of them by Paul and his associates: "Are we beginning to commend ourselves again? Or do we need, as some do, letters of recommendation to you, or from you?" (2 Cor 3:1). Such letters were important because they assured the recipients that the bearer of the letter was trustworthy. Paul did not have formal authority over Jesus groups in Rome (Rom 1:13-15). He had had nothing to do with their organization or membership, and as far as they were concerned, Paul was a complete outsider. According to Bruce J. Malina and John J. Pilch, for Paul to write a letter of recommendation to Jesus groups that he did not know would be very presumptuous, even downright dishonorable.[27] Because he was an outsider, Paul would not have been recognized by them as a broker or intermediary with the right to introduce Phoebe to them. In fact, a letter from an outsider would have functioned as a huge insult. Paul knew better than to do such a thing. Notice how very early on in Romans he takes pains to avoid insulting them. He states that he hopes to impart some spiritual gift to them (1:11) but quickly adds that they too will strengthen him (1:12).

Both Paul and Phoebe were well aware that since Paul was not personally known to Jesus groups in Rome, a letter of recommendation from him would have been worthless, in fact, more of a liability to Phoebe than an aid. This is strong evidence in support of the thesis that Paul's recommendation of Phoebe was not intended for Rome. Ephesus, therefore, is a more likely candidate for the destination of Romans 16:1-23. One can easily imagine Paul writing a letter of recommendation for Phoebe, who was intending to visit Ephesus. Ephesus was located due east of Kenchreai across the Aegean Sea, and Paul was well acquainted with members of its Jesus groups (Acts 18:19-21; 19:1-8, 17, 26-27; 1 Cor 16:8-9). Since it is inconceivable that Paul would have sent such a letter to Rome, we will not join those who imagine Phoebe to be the bearer of the letter to the Romans to Jesus groups in Rome. Instead, we will envision her as the bearer of a letter of recommendation written for her by Paul, a letter that she needed to secure assistance from Christ-believers living in Ephesus.

Ephesus was one of the oldest settlements near the Aegean Sea on the western coast of Asia Minor (present-day Turkey). In Paul's day it served as the provincial seat of the Roman government in Asia Minor. In ancient times, the city of Ephesus was an important port through which goods were exported to western locations, to regions that we call Italy and Greece. Ephesus was an important cultic center that gave pride of place to Artemis and Apollo who, according to tradition, were born there.[28] Moreover, it housed a magnificent temple dedicated to Artemis and was known as the foremost site where the earth goddess was worshiped.

According to Luke (Acts 19:23-41), Paul caused great consternation for silversmiths in Ephesus whose livelihoods derived from the creation of souvenir silver shrines of Artemis. Apparently his proclamation of the gospel of Christ was turning so many people away from Artemis that the silversmiths were losing considerable business. Their livelihoods were in jeopardy, and they were understandably furious with Paul. A riot ensued, in which Paul's traveling companions, Gaius and Aristarchus, were dragged into the theatre by the crowd. Fortunately for them, the *grammateus* (secretary, chief executive officer) put an end to the incident.

Ephesus was a strategic city in the growth of Jesus groups. According to Luke, Paul spent either two years and three months (Acts 19:8-10) or three years (20:31) there. During that time, Ephesus served as a center from which the word of God was brought to many residents in Asia Minor (19:10). Luke tells us nothing about the composition of Jesus groups in Ephesus. In fact, his only reference to Christ-believers in Ephesus mentions twelve disciples who had received John's baptism of repentance and whom Paul later baptized in the name of Jesus (19:1-7). With a number of others, however, we argue that Ephesus is more likely the destination of Romans 16:1-23 than Rome. If this is correct, these verses reveal important information about the shape of Jesus groups in Ephesus.

Paul identifies Priscilla[29] and Aquila as "my fellow-workers in Christ Jesus, who risked their necks for my life, to whom not only I but also all the churches of the Gentiles give thanks" (Rom 16:3-4). That Prisca and Aquila are mentioned first in the list of greetings (Rom 16:3-16), suggests that they were important associates in Paul's work of proclaiming the gospel of God's raising Jesus from the dead in view of a forthcoming Israelite theocracy. Furthermore, their household was one of the meeting places for Christ-believers (Rom 16:5). In reference to this group, Paul uses the word *ekklēsia*, a Greek word usually translated as "church." Today, we often think of "church" as the building where Christians gather for worship. This was not so for Paul. *Ekklēsia* refers to the congregation or assembly; it means the people, a gathering of believers. To avoid the association of first-century assemblies of Christ-believers with buildings, it is preferable to refer to these "churches" as Jesus groups.[30]

Paul mentions additional Jesus groups in chapter 16 of Romans. He greets believers in the households of Aristobulus (Rom 16:10) and Narcissus (16:11). He also mentions "Asyncritus, Phlegon, Hermes, Patrobas, Hermas, and the brethren who are with them" (16:14). The Greek word for "brother" is *adelphos*. Since the plural form (*adelphoi*) can mean both brothers and sisters,[31] we must imagine these "brothers" as members of a Jesus group comprised of both men and women. The next verse mentions a number of male and female Christ-believers and "all the saints who are with them" (16:15). When the Greek word for "saint" (*hagios*) is used in the plural (*hagioi*), it refers to a group of individuals who belong exclusively to God, here, a group of Christ-believers.

Conclusion

Unlike Phoebe Snow, Phoebe of Kenchreai is not a fictitious character, created for commercial purposes. She is listed among a number of individuals whom St. Paul knew either personally or by reputation. His letter of recommendation (Rom 16:1-2) identifies her as *adelphē* (sister), *diakonos* (arguably, deacon), and *prostatis* (patron). With a view to getting to know Phoebe, we shall attempt to understand what these words meant to people living in the Mediterranean region in the first century AD. What information does Paul convey to his addressees when he calls Phoebe "our sister" (chapter 1)? Was there anything special about the town of Kenchreai (chapter 2)? What role did a *diakonos* (chapter 3) or a *prostatis* (chapter 4) play in the lives of first-century Mediterranean people? We will see that although Paul uses only a few words to describe Phoebe, they provide glimpses into her social status, her relationship with Paul, and her role in the first-century Jesus groups of Kenchreai and Ephesus.

CHAPTER 1

Phoebe, Our Sister

Paul's mention of Phoebe comes in a typical first-century letter of recommendation directed to the Ephesians (Rom 16:1-2). The form of this letter includes a request verb, the name of the individual being recommended, the individual's credentials, and a request.[1] Paul commences with the verb *sunistēmi*, which means "I introduce" or "I recommend." The intention of this verb is to request something. By recommending Phoebe to Ephesian Christ-believers, Paul signals his approval of her; his implicit request is that the recipients adopt the same attitude. Paul then states her name and identifies her as a *diakonos* (usually translated as "deacon") and *prostatis* ("patron"). The letter of recommendation closes with his overt request that members of the Jesus groups in Ephesus receive her as one of them and give her whatever assistance she may need. Such letters of recommendation were important in first-century collectivist Mediterranean societies, and this one most likely went a long way toward assuring the warmth of Phoebe's welcome.

Generally speaking, societies can be described as either collectivistic or individualistic.[2] American and Canadian societies tend to be individualistic while Mediterranean societies are collectivistic. Those of us raised in individualistic societies know that we emphasize the individual, personal goals, and personal achievements. Collectivistic societies, however, place more importance on groups than on individuals, the primary group being one's family. Within such societies, children soon learn that a meaningful human existence requires reliance on the family and that the needs of the family take priority over their personal goals and interests. They also learn that allegiance to the village group and membership in its related associations are vital to a happy life. A collectivist's sense of self and identity derives from his or her relationships within these significant groups, especially the family.

A core cultural value that holds collectivistic families together is group attachment (also called "love"), and love manifests itself through loyalty toward other family members. This loyalty involves a number of features. Those who love the family do what the family values. Moreover, they defer to parental authority and will not disobey their parents in public because doing so would shame the entire family. Collectivists value authority and prefer hierarchical relationships; equality is not a collectivistic value. Nor do collectivists emphasize youth and productivity over age and being. For them, honor increases with age and being is more important than doing. While advertising sells the *new* in individualistic societies, collectivists prefer that which is rooted in tradition.

The bonds between members of a collectivistic family are deeply rooted, and it is essential to note that it is in a collectivistic context—not an individualistic context—that Phoebe arrives with her recommendation from Paul. In the opening of his letter, Paul immediately uses kinship terminology to identify her. Phoebe is "our sister." While it is true that spouses, colleagues, and members of the same associations or tribes sometimes referred to one another as "brother" or "sister,"[3] these kinship terms first of all signified biological siblings. The primary context in which those who hear Paul's recommendation read aloud is that of the collectivistic family.

Siblings in Collectivistic Families

When Paul designates Phoebe as "our sister," he means that she is not only *his* sister but also the sister of Jesus-group members, that is, every Christ-believer in Ephesus. And since the word "sister" is very familiar to us, we naturally think that we know what Paul means by it. But remember, Paul and Phoebe lived in a first-century Mediterranean collectivist context; thus, their experience of family relationships was vastly different from ours. In order to comprehend what Paul means by "our sister," we must grasp how first-century Mediterraneans understood sibling relationships within biological families. Only then can we proceed to a correct understanding of how sibling terminology functioned within the Jesus movement.

The Bible abounds with stories about families that continue to speak powerfully to Christians today. Contemporary sermons on the well-known parable of the Prodigal Son (Luke 15:11-32), for example, often focus on relationships within families, especially relationships between parents and children and among siblings. While there is pastoral wisdom in this approach, many of us—preachers included—think that the family that Luke is describing is much like our own, a nuclear family consisting of a married man and woman, along with their children. What many fail to realize is that Luke is not describing a nuclear family. Those who first heard this parable belonged to extended families that usually consisted of a man, his wife (or wives), his unmarried daughters, and all of his sons, their wives, and their children.[4] They often lived in the same dwelling or in a number of adjoining dwellings and worked together to provide life's necessities for the family. Their common property was controlled by the eldest male. While he symbolized the family to the outside world and was ultimately responsible for its public reputation, every member of the household was obliged to do whatever was necessary to protect the family's reputation, in other words, their honor rating. Honor was much sought after by the people who populate the pages of the Bible. In fact, honor was—and still is—the highest Mediterranean-area value. It played an integral role not only in how people understood their own behavior but also in how they behaved toward others.

Honor is defined as the positive value of a person in his or her own eyes and must be publicly acknowledged.[5] There is no such thing as honor that is not publicly recognized. Anthropologists identify two kinds of honor in Mediterranean societies: ascribed and acquired honor.[6] Ascribed honor is the honor with which one is born. Birth into elite families brought with it a great deal of ascribed honor, while birth into poor families brought much less. Regardless of one's social status, however, one's family always possessed a measure of ascribed honor, which was usually maintained from generation to generation. Acquired honor, meanwhile, was gained by males who were able to outwit their peers in public situations of challenge and response. A subtle insult was made. Its recipient had to realize that he had been insulted and how seriously. He then had to respond in kind if he wished to maintain his honor rating and that of his family. There were also positive challenges, such as compliments or gifts. Again, the individual had to respond appropriately in order to save face for himself and his family. This public game of challenge and response was a critical part of everyday life; failing to respond or being outwitted by another meant loss of honor, something that every family strove diligently to avoid.

Shame works in tandem with honor and needs to be addressed at the same time. As with the concept of honor, there are two kinds of shame, one negative and the other positive. Negative shame results when one claims a personal pride that is publicly denied.[7] For example, the one who is outwitted by another in public (challenge and response) loses honor; he and his family are publicly and negatively shamed. Positive shame, however, has to do with one's concern to safeguard one's honor and therefore the honor of one's family. Unmarried women who safeguard their virginity until marriage, and married women who conduct themselves chastely, demonstrate positive shame because by their good conduct, they are protecting the family's public reputation.

Members of individualistic societies also enjoy honors and try to avoid being publicly shamed (often called "embarrassment"). These values do not play out in the same way as they do in collectivistic societies. Individualists are much more likely, for example, to reject the idea that the reputation of the entire family is tarnished when one of its members fails to meet society's expectations, while in collectivistic societies the behavior of one member of the family affects the reputation of the entire family, for good or for bad.

Thus, first-century extended families clearly differed from today's nuclear families in form and function. They also interacted with the world outside the household in a manner foreign to most of us. Members of the household belonged to the same ingroup, a term that anthropologists use to refer to groups sharing similar values. Groups with whom they perceive themselves to be in competition are called outgroups.[8] While members of the same ingroup are bound together by a spirit of solidarity and loyalty, they compete with outsiders to gain honor. Moreover, they take measures to ensure that they will not lose honor. Information that might prove damaging to a family's reputation is kept secret to prevent outsiders from making it public knowledge.[9]

In general, then, collectivistic families are very concerned about what other people think of them, so much so that, for them, the parable of the Prodigal Son is not primarily about severed family relationships and the need for forgiveness to restore harmony within the household. For them, the parable speaks primarily about a family's relationship with the rest of the village. Luke states that the father has divided his resources between his two sons (Luke 15:12). What this means is that each son has accepted his share of the inheritance while his father is still alive. By doing so, both sons grievously offend their father and publicly disgrace him. For collectivists, this parable is about how the greed of two sons destroys a family's honor rating in the eyes of their neighbors.[10] The wasteful behavior of the younger son and the elder son's refusal to join in the feast heaps shame upon the father, and consequently, upon the entire household. The parable serves, therefore, as a warning against self-seeking behavior that could easily destroy a family's honor.

Seldom, if ever, do contemporary preachers interpret the parable through the cultural lens of honor. Instead, most assume that biblical families looked like contemporary families, operated in the same way, and valued the same things. As I have indicated, such ideas are false. The roles that family members played, relationships among them, and their attitudes toward outsiders do not equate with those of American or Canadian Christians today. Even the words "father," "mother," "sister," and "brother" symbolize roles that played out in ways foreign to us. Simply put, the familiar concept of "family," featured in so many biblical passages, has little in common with family life as it is now lived in most twenty-first-century North American and northern European societies. For this reason, and I must emphasize this point, we cannot fully appreciate Phoebe's role as "our sister" until we understand how the ancients understood the terms "sister" and "brother."

Although the concept of family is becoming increasingly complex in North America, we still tend to think of brothers and sisters as individuals who have the same biological mother and father. Biblical authors did not share our view. Recall, for example, when Abraham and Sarah live as foreigners in Gerar, and Abraham gives Sarah to King Abimelech out of fear for his own life (Gen 20:11). The couple tells the king that they are brother and sister. When Abimelech realizes that Sarah is also Abraham's wife, he demands that Abraham account for his actions, which have provoked God's wrath against the king (20:1-18). In his own defense, Abraham replies, "She is indeed my sister, the daughter of my father but not the daughter of my mother; and she became my wife" (20:12). Abraham's response is telling. He and Sarah are doubly related: they are husband and wife, and they are also biological brother and sister, having the same father but different mothers. When children share one parent, we refer to them today as "half" brother and sister. This terminology is foreign to biblical authors. As far as the author of this story is concerned, Sarah is not Abraham's *half sister*. She is his *sister* because she has the same biological father as Abraham; the identity of their mothers is immaterial.

This understanding of what constituted siblings is visible elsewhere in the Bible. Consider the sons of Jacob. They are always designated brothers (Gen 37:4-5, 9-14, 16, 26-27) even though Jacob has two wives (Leah and Rachel) and two concubines (Zilpah and Bilhah). Moreover, Solomon, the son of Bathsheba, is the brother of Adonijah, the son of Haggith (1 Kgs 1:10; 2:15, 21-22) and the brother of Absalom (2:7), the son of Maacah (2 Sam 3:3). In each case, David is the father and even though these men have different mothers, they are portrayed as brothers.

New Testament authors convey the same understanding of what constitutes siblings. In the genealogies of Jesus (Matt 1:1-16; Luke 3:23-38), for example, we hear over and over again of how men beget children. Only four women are named in Matthew's genealogy and not a single woman is mentioned in Luke's. For the ancients, the father was the active agent in procreation because the male seed was considered to be a miniature replica of the child to be born. Thus his children belonged to him because he begat them. The mother was simply the vessel that nurtured the developing baby.[11] Children born to her were not deemed brothers and sisters unless they had the same father. This is an important piece of information because stories about biological families abound in the Bible, and if we are to interpret them in a way that respects the understanding of their writers, a culturally correct understanding of kinship terms is necessary. While Paul does not refer to biological siblings when he calls Phoebe "our sister" (Rom 16:1), the notion that sisters and brothers are children of the same father lies, as we shall see, beneath his claim.

Fictive Kinship

So far we have been talking about biological kinship. There is, however, another type of kinship, one that accounts for Paul's designation of Phoebe as "our sister." Anthropologists have learned that in different societies, the terms for mother, father, sister, brother, and so on, are not restricted to members of the same biological family. They may refer, for example, to aspects of nature; this is true of expressions such as "Mother Earth."[12] Kinship terms may also be used in reference to members of the same clan, tribe, or extended kin group (Gen 13:8; Exod 2:11; Lev 25:35-39; Deut 15:7, 9, 11-12; 22:1-4).[13] Kinship language can even extend to individuals who are not related by marriage or by blood, a phenomenon that anthropologists classify as a type of pseudo-kinship known as fictive kinship.[14] In these cases, unrelated individuals are given statuses similar to that of one's biological or affinal (related by marriage) kin. Paul's reference to Phoebe as "our sister" is an example of fictive kinship terminology.

Family Ties and the Jesus Movement

The canonical gospels recount stories of the separation of individuals from their families to follow Jesus. Mark's account of the call of the first disciples of Jesus is an excellent example. Prompted by the invitation of Jesus, Simon and Andrew leave their nets and follow him (Mark 1:16-18). Jesus then calls James and John, the sons of Zebedee. The brothers respond immediately, leaving their father behind in the boat with the hired servants (1:19-20). It is easy for individualists to grossly underestimate the drama of these scenes. The fact that the father of James and John is left behind with only hired servants means that James and John are his only sons. By depriving the rest of their family of their protection and support, the young men jeopardize their chances of survival. Moreover, honor of one's parents was of paramount importance in Mediterranean culture (Exod 21:15, 17; Lev 20:9; Sir 3:1-11), superseded only by the command to honor God. The Roman historian Plutarch (AD 46–120) expressed what every child was taught about the duty to honor one's parents:

> For through philosophy and in company with philosophy
> it is possible to attain knowledge of what is honorable and
> what is shameful, what is just and what is unjust, what, in
> brief, is to be chosen and what to be avoided, how a man
> must bear himself in his relations with the gods, with his
> parents, with his elders, with the laws, with strangers, with
> those in authority, with friends, with women, with children,
> with servants; that one ought to reverence the gods, to
> honor one's parents, to respect one's elders, to be obedient
> to the laws, to yield to those in authority, to love one's
> friends, to be chaste with women, to be affectionate with
> children, and not to be overbearing with slaves. (Plutarch,
> The Education of Children, 7.D-E) [15]

Ideally, a son followed in his father's footsteps. He learned his
father's trade and looked after his parents in their old age. A
daughter married and bore children, preferably sons, who would
support her and her husband in their old age. If a son left family
behind in order to join something like Jesus' faction, this would
be considered deviant behavior unless the father urged him to
join for the benefit of the family (see Matt 20:20 where the mother
of the sons of Zebedee sees such a benefit). But if parents were
opposed, this would be deviant behavior[16] because it meant that
these children would not be able to fulfill their obligations to
their parents. One of the most sacred obligations of children was
to provide for the burial of their parents. Failure to do so was to
reject family loyalties that had been strongly reinforced since
childhood. One New Testament passage deals with this very
issue: "Another of the disciples said to him, 'Lord, let me first go
and bury my father.' But Jesus said to him, 'Follow me, and leave
the dead to bury their own dead'" (Matt 8:21-22). Try to imagine
the impact of this statement in light of the fact that honor of one's
parents was sacrosanct. Those who abandoned their parents and
their family responsibilities (as James and John did) brought great
dishonor upon themselves and their families.

While love and honor of one's parents was the social ideal, it
is recorded in the gospels that Jesus actually told people to hate

their parents: "If anyone comes to me and does not hate his own father and mother and wife and children and brothers and sisters, yes, and even his own life, he cannot be my disciple" (Luke 14:26). These words are shocking to contemporary Christians. Did Jesus actually promote feelings of hatred toward one's parents? In the Bible, to *hate* is the same as to separate oneself from others. Therefore, to depart from one's family for any reason was to hate father, mother, wife, and children.[17] When entire households joined Jesus groups (Acts 16:31-34), disciples could remain attached to their families. But this was not always the case. Sometimes not all members of a family joined the Jesus group (Luke 9:57-62), and this meant that those who did severed ties with their biological families. Leaving everything for the sake of Jesus and the gospel meant that one was now attached to Jesus and his group members rather than to one's family. In the above passage, Jesus is not telling his listeners to harbor feelings of hatred toward members of their biological families. Rather, he is saying that to become his disciples their primary loyalty has to be to him and to the family of disciples rather than to their biological families. Nevertheless, in a world where family loyalty is everything, the decision to abandon one's family for the sake of the gospel incurs great personal cost. Simon will still have his brother Andrew, and James will still have John, but ties with their respective families are severed by following Jesus.

The Formation of a New Family

As each of the canonical gospels progresses, conflict intensifies between Jesus and the political-religious authorities. As early as the second chapter of Mark, Jesus is already butting heads with the scribes over the question of who can declare sins forgiven by God (Mark 2:6-12). Purity rules become an issue when Jesus eats with tax collectors and sinners (2:15-17), and Torah interpretation adds to the growing list of controversies when the Pharisees discover Jesus' disciples plucking heads of grain on the Sabbath

(2:23-28). Chapter 3 of Mark opens with the story of the man with a withered hand (3:1-6; this passage concludes a set of five begun in Mark 2:1). In light of previous clashes with the political-religious authorities, Jesus expects another public challenge to his honor. His sense of shame (desire to protect his honor) is so acute by now that he does not wait for his opponents to question him. The fact that they are watching him to see what he will do already constitutes a challenge to his honor. They need not say anything. Jesus takes the lead, asking the Pharisees whether it is lawful "to do good or to do harm, to save life or to kill" on the Sabbath (3:4). As Jesus well knows, work on the Sabbath is not permitted (Lev 23:3; Jer 17:21-22). But he frames the incident in terms of doing good deeds and saving lives. He then heals the man, again demonstrating his prowess in the game of challenge and response. His opponents, defeated once more, plot with the monarchists, the Herodians, about how to destroy him (Mark 3:6). Significantly, to opt for violence is to lose the game of challenge and response; hence, their choice signals their decisive defeat.[18]

As tensions mount between Jesus and the political-religious authorities, his reputation escalates among the crowds who flock to him for healing (Mark 3:8). All this attention becomes known to his biological family members who are embarrassed by his behavior. They set out to bring him home (3:21): "And his mother and his brothers came; and standing outside they sent to him and called him. And a crowd was sitting about him; and they said to him; 'Your mother and your brothers are outside asking for you.' And he replied, 'Who are my mother and my brothers?' And looking around on those who sat about him, he said, 'Here are my mother and my brothers! Whoever does the will of God is my brother, and sister, and mother'" (Mark 3:31-35). Jesus does not go home with his family. Instead, he redefines what it means to be family—it is those who do God's will who constitute his family. In Matthew's version of this story, Jesus points at his disciples, indicating that it is they who do God's will and thus, they constitute his new family (Matt 12:49-50). In the context of his prophetic proclamation of God's forthcoming theocracy,

Jesus' faction was a political-religious faction. His disciples were recruited to assist him in spreading the news of this forthcoming kingdom. His audience was his "brothers," or other Israelites. The institutional context was political-religious Israel.

But after Jesus' death and resurrection, the institutional context soon changes. For Paul, the framework is no longer political-religious but domestic-religious, a fictive kin group of believers in the God of Israel who raised Jesus from the dead. In turn, the category "disciple" shifted from helper of Jesus to follower of Jesus. "Brother/sister" was no longer member of the house of Israel, but member of Jesus groups. We can trace this change in the book of Acts, and its realization in the letters of Paul.

Thus after Jesus' death and resurrection, we are informed by the writer of Acts of how the number of his "disciples," meaning more than the original Twelve, grew (Acts 2:41-42). As time went on, members of early Jesus groups appropriated kinship terms to describe their newfound relationships in Jesus. Evidence of this occurs in Paul's usage of the term *adelphos*, meaning "brother" (Rom 14:10; 1 Cor 1:1; 2 Cor 1:1; Phil 2:25; 1 Thess 3:2; Phlm 1) and *adelphē*, meaning "sister" (Rom 16:15; 1 Cor 7:15; 9:5; Phlm 2). Since Paul is usually addressing entire assemblies in his letters, however, the kinship term that he uses most frequently is *adelphoi* (Rom 1:13; 1 Cor 10:1; 2 Cor 1:8; Gal 1:2; 6:1; Phil 1:12; 1 Thess 2:1), the plural form of "brother." When used to address mixed audiences, *adelphoi* includes women and means both brothers and sisters.[19] This is usually the case when Paul is addressing Jesus groups, because their ranks included men as well as women (1 Cor 7:1-16; 9:4; 11:1-16; 14:34-35).

Paul's use of kinship terminology is rooted in his conviction that all who are baptized in Christ form a new house of Israel, just as previously the old house of Israel included those born "in Israel" (Israel is another name for Jacob). Now all brothers and sisters who are baptized into Jesus' death also share in his resurrection: "Do you not know that all of us who have been baptized into Christ Jesus were baptized into his death? We were buried with him therefore by baptism into death, so that as Christ was raised from the dead by the glory of the Father, we too might walk in newness of life. For if we have been united with him in a death like his, we shall certainly be united with him in a resurrection like his" (Rom 6:3-5). Paul also teaches that the Spirit of the Father who raised Jesus from the dead dwells in the gathering of believers and gives life to them (Rom 8:11). Through that same Spirit, believers become collective adopted children and heirs of God (Rom 8:14-17). As children of God, they are brothers and sisters of Christ and of one another (Rom 8:29).

The primary relationship among members of the Jesus movement was, in fact, that of brother and sister, a relationship that held deep significance for them even before they joined the group. In first-century Mediterranean societies, biological brothers and sisters grew up in patriarchal households. They spent their early years primarily in the company of women who ran the household: grandmothers, mothers, elder sisters, sisters-in-law. This form of child rearing (called the "father-absent family") produced brothers and sisters tied very closely by bonds of loyalty and affection,[20] an emotional intimacy that tended to remain throughout their lives.

While maintaining the importance of the brother-sister bond, as culturally expected, Jesus, and Paul after him, set aside the structure of the patriarchal family, which governed families. Since the groups formed by Jesus and Paul were not actual kinship groups, their fictive kin groups adopted the usual structure of a mother's-brother-archy, a secondary structure in a patriarchal society that covered relationships among males and females in the matriline. The result was a kind of family of voluntary membership, headed by males without legal entitlements or rights. While people joined, they could just as easily leave (not the case with the patriarchal family). Since institutions are social ways to realize values, the Jesus groups as fictive kin groups sought to realize values such as service to one another and commitment to God.[21] Therefore, although joining a Jesus group often meant loss of connection with one's biological family, family remained a central focus of one's life. In short, Jesus groups formed surrogate or fictive families.[22] Their members were to relate with the affection of biological brothers and sisters and to exercise loyalty and commitment to the God of Israel.[23] In contrast to the practice in traditional households with their patriarchs and their rights and entitlements, fictive kin groups had as their head individuals with the role of the mother's brother (a matrilineal uncle, in medieval English called an "Em"), a male without rights, the male who related to a mother's children because of his attachment to the mother. This is a mother's-brother-archy, or uncle-archy, focused in group attachment, concern for group members, yet without rights over the group or any entitlements. In Jesus groups, no human individual assumed the role of patriarch or biological father. Rather, God was the head of these households. Members of the community were to be brothers and sisters under the care of one father, God.

Paul identifies Phoebe as "our sister" (Rom 16:1) to underscore that she shares an intimate bond with every member of the Jesus group regardless of where they are located. As a disciple of Jesus, she is one of them, their *sister*. Because of this, she deserves the love and care that biological siblings owe one another and that every member of the Jesus-movement groups now owe to every other member. Even though Jesus groups in Ephesus are meeting Phoebe for the first time when she arrives with her letter of introduction, she is already an insider because she belongs to the same fictive family.

CHAPTER 2

Phoebe of Kenchreai

Home to more than ten million people, Greece is located in southern Europe between Albania on the west and Turkey on the east. The country is comprised of three sections: the mainland, located just south of the Balkan countries of Albania and Bulgaria; the Peloponnesus, the southernmost peninsula that has technically been an island since 1893 when the canal cutting through the Isthmus of Corinth was completed; and the approximately three thousand islands that belong to Greece, the largest being Crete. Much of Greece is surrounded by water: the Mediterranean Sea to the south, the Ionian Sea on the west, and the Aegean Sea on the east. Only one-fifth of its total land mass (130,800 square kilometers) is arable, yielding crops such as wheat, barley, corn, and olives. Greece is one of numerous countries located in a vast geographical region that anthropologists refer to as the Mediterranean culture continent.[1] There are other culture continents in the world, but this particular one includes every country that borders on the Mediterranean Sea, as well as Portugal, which does not. It therefore comprises countries of the Middle East, North Africa, and Southern Europe.

A culture continent (or culture area) is a part of the earth's surface on which groups of people share similar cultural characteristics.[2] They may, for example, speak the same or related languages and form similar types of social organizations and lifestyles. Climate is thought to be an important factor in the development of a culture continent. The Mediterranean climate is arid; the summers are hot and dry, and precipitation is limited to a few winter months. This rainfall pattern affects soil conditions and largely determines the kinds of vegetation capable of survival, not to mention the crops that can be successfully cultivated. This, in turn, affects the culture of the region's inhabitants—how they live as much as what they eat. In any geographical region, when comparable climate conditions persist for many centuries, inhabitants tend to develop similar cultivation and settlement patterns; similar lifestyles lead to the development of shared cultural traits. In the last chapter, we talked about how the cultural values of honor and shame play out in collectivistic families. Within the Mediterranean culture continent, partly as a result of the climatic conditions that necessitated that groups work together to survive, the collectivistic family prevailed, and the core cultural values of honor and shame permeated relationships on all levels. Honor was rigorously sought and jealously protected.[3] The first-century town of Kenchreai, like many other towns in the Mediterranean region to this very day, was populated by collectivistic people whose concern for honor, both individual and familial, permeated relationships on a daily basis.

Ancient Corinth

In Phoebe's lifetime, Kenchreai was closely connected with the city-state known as Corinth. Settled no later than 4000 BC, Corinth became the most famous and influential city of the Corinthia, an area of approximately nine hundred square kilometers that included land on both sides of the Isthmus of Corinth, stretching from Megara (just northeast of the Isthmus of Corinth)

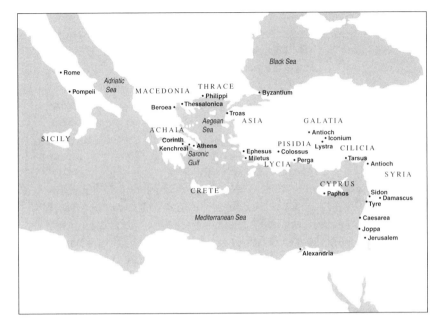

Figure 1: Southeastern Roman Empire in First Century

to as far south as Epidaurus on the eastern side of the Peloponnesus.[4] According to legend, Corinth was founded and ruled by
an order of kings, notably Sisyphus, whose efforts established
Corinth as a major center.

Located on the Isthmus of Corinth—a small strip of land only
seven kilometers wide at its narrowest point—the city of Corinth
was in a strategic spot. It was there that the major roads between
the Peloponnesian Peninsula and the mainland (of the country
we call Greece today) met, as well as the sea routes between the
eastern and western Mediterranean. Since Corinth lay on the
chief north-south route, it naturally became a center for trade,
controlling commerce between Italy and Asia Minor, and between the mainland and the Peloponnesian Peninsula. The abundance of its water supply and the fertility of its land also
contributed to Corinth's prominence.[5] The most striking physical
feature of the city's district was the 575-meter-tall limestone

mountain called the Acrocorinth, which functioned as Corinth's citadel from at least the fourth century BC.[6] The area's most fertile land lay just west of the Acrocorinth.

In approximately 1000 BC, the Dorians of Argos settled in Corinth[7] and developed ceramics and shipbuilding, which greatly contributed to commerce in that area. In the eighth century BC, the Dorian Bacchiad clan usurped the power of the Corinthian kings and assumed command, eventually turning Corinth into a strong military site.[8] The Bacchiadae were defeated in 657 BC and replaced by the tyrant Kypselos, a native prince, who ruled for thirty years, during which time he strengthened Corinth's position as a center of trade. He was succeeded by his son Periander, whose rule has been thought of as a golden age in Corinth's history. After Periander's death, Corinth began to decline slowly. In 338 BC, Philip of Macedon, the father of Alexander the Great, conquered Corinth and, in time, it was revitalized and prosperous once again. Then, in 146 BC, the Hellenistic city-state of Corinth was overtaken and destroyed by the Romans. For approximately a century, Corinth was devastated, but not abandoned; in 44 BC Julius Caesar initiated its rebuilding. Corinth was recolonized by freedmen and named *Laus Julia Corinthus* in honor of its new patron.[9] Corinth, once a Hellenistic ("Greek") city, was now a Roman colony that, no doubt, was visited often by Paul and Phoebe.

During the Hellenistic and Roman periods, the two major ports that served the city of Corinth were the western port, Lechaeum, located on the Gulf of Corinth less than two kilometers north of Corinth, and the eastern port, Kenchreai, located on the Saronic Gulf almost nine kilometers east of Corinth. By controlling the movement of goods between the two gulfs, Kenchreai and Lechaeum served not only Corinth but most of the Peloponnesian Peninsula. Kenchreai facilitated trade with the Eastern Mediterranean, especially Asia Minor and Egypt, while Lechaeum served trade to the west.[10] The Corinthia was famous for its bronze works and pottery. Perfumes and textiles were also produced in abundance. Many of these products were

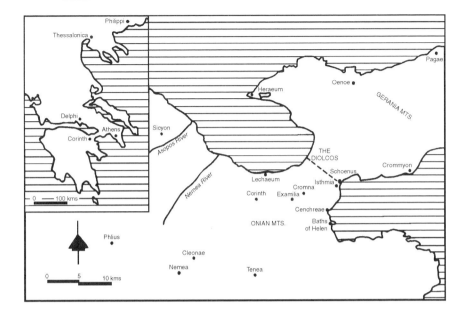

Figure 2: Map of the Corinthia

exported and made their way to Italy via Lechaeum and to Asia
Minor via Kenchreai.

The Port of Kenchreai

Today's Greek village of Kechries, located at the foot of Mount
Oneion in the Peloponnesus Peninsula, is in the vicinity of
Phoebe's Kenchreai whose remains lie partly under water.
Kenchreai is first mentioned by the historian Thucydides in con-
nection with the attack of the Athenians on Corinth in 425 BC:

> As for the Athenians, when the enemy no longer came
> against them and offered battle, they stripped the corpses,
> took up their own dead, and straightway set up a trophy.
> Meanwhile the other half of the Corinthian forces, which
> was stationed at Cenchreae as a garrison to prevent the

> Athenians from making a descent upon Crommyon, were
> unable to see the battle because Mount Oneium intervened;
> but when they saw the cloud of dust and realized what
> was going on, they rushed thither at once, as did also the
> older men in the city of Corinth when they perceived what
> had happened. (*The Peloponnesian War*, 4.44.2-4)[11]

Centuries later, when the Romans rebuilt Corinth (44 BC), a
new port of Kenchreai was constructed not far from the previous
Hellenistic port.[12] Roman Kenchreai had a natural harbor. Although there were other harbors along the Saronic coast, most
were small and too far away from the more highly populated
areas to attract much use.[13] Kenchreai's oval harbor was situated
only ten kilometers due east of the agora (marketplace) of Corinth
and served ships coming from Athens, Ionia, Cyprus, and the
rest of the Levant (the middle part of the Fertile Crescent, between the Nile Valley and present-day Iraq). It was at this time
that two new moles (breakwaters), constructed out of earth,
rubble, and rock, were added to guarantee a deep-water port.[14]
Roman Kenchreai even had docks for the large war fleet of the
Corinthian city-state. Thus, thanks to the Roman rebuilding project, in Phoebe's lifetime, Kenchreai was once again a major port,[15]
serving as one of the main doors between the Peloponnesus and
the East. Its inhabitants had easy access to excellent agricultural
land and to all the amenities available to residents of Corinth.[16]
A major road connected Kenchreai and Corinth; one could make
the journey by foot in approximately two hours.

While the east and south sides of Kenchreai were protected by
water and the west by rocky ledges, there was no natural means
of defense to the north. Archeological excavations conducted from
1963–1968 uncovered remains of a limestone wall that guarded
the north side, a wall that appears to date back to at least the
fourth century BC.[17] Remains of the ancient harbor, particularly
the relatively small basin and structures around it, are still visible
to excavators. While its exact dimensions are unknown, indications are that it was approximately thirty thousand square meters
in size.[18] The harbor offered anchorage that was well sheltered

from the prevailing northeast wind. The northwest and southwest harbor-side commercial facilities included a number of warehouses and shops. Warehouse facilities existed in the central area of the port, and there was another commercial district further inland.[19] The residential section of Kenchreai, approximately one kilometer east to west and 365 meters north to south, overlooked the inner harbor. This was the Kenchreai Phoebe knew.

The Diolkos

An important reference to ancient Kenchreai survives in Strabo's *Geographia*. Strabo, a Hellenistic geographer and historian, was born in 64 or 63 BC in the city of Amasia, the royal residence of the kings of Pontus. Strabo spent his life in travel and study. He was at Corinth in 44 and 29 BC, lived in Alexandria, Egypt, from 25–20 BC, settled at Rome after AD 14, and died in approximately AD 23.[20] His seventeen-volume *Geographia* has survived almost completely intact and is of great value because of his extensive observations. It contains historical material as well as descriptions of places and peoples and is a rich source of knowledge of the ancient world. Writing in Greek in a world dominated by Rome, Strabo had this to say about Corinthian commerce:

> Corinth is called wealthy because of its commerce, since it is situated on the Isthmus and is master of two harbors, of which the one leads straight to Asia, and the other to Italy; and it makes easy the exchange of merchandise for both countries that are so far distant from each other. And just as in early times the Strait of Sicily was not easy to navigate, so also the high seas, and particularly the sea beyond Maleae, were not, on account of the contrary winds; and hence the proverb, "But when you double Maleae, forget your home." At any rate, it was a welcome alternative, for the merchants both from Italy and from Asia, to avoid the voyage to Maleae and to land their cargoes here. . . . The beginning of the seaboard on the two sides is, on one side

Lechaion and on the other, Cenchreae, a village and a harbor distant about seventy stadia from Corinth. Now this latter they use for the trade from Asia, but Lechaeum for that from Italy. . . . The shore that extends from here [Lechaeum] to Pagae in Megaris is washed by the Corinthian Gulf. It is concave and with the shore on the other side, at Schoenus which is near Cenchreae, it forms the "Diolkos." (Strabo, *Geography*, viii, 6, 20, 22)[21]

What is this "Diolkos" that Strabo mentions? The Greek verb *holkazō* means "to draw along, to drag."[22] Basically, then, the Diolkos was a paved roadway of almost sixteen kilometers built across the Isthmus of Corinth to transport vessels and cargo between the Corinthian Gulf and the Saronic Gulf.[23] On its Saronic Gulf side, the Diolkos ended at the port of Schoenus, only eight kilometers from Kenchreai. It is not known whether there was a settlement where the Diolkos ended on the Corinthian Gulf side. The large paving stones that formed it began right at the water's edge. While the loading area was approximately ten meters wide, the remainder of the Diolkos ranged from 3.6 to 4.2 meters wide.[24] Ships were first unloaded so as to reduce the weight; they were then dragged onto the Diolkos. A movable wooden platform or *holkos* was used to transport them over the roadway, its wheels guided by tracks cut into the stones. The unloaded cargo was transported to the other end of the isthmus via the normal roads. Once the ship had been dragged across the isthmus, its cargo was reloaded and it went once again on its way. One can only imagine what an enormous asset the Diolkos was to trade in and beyond the Peloponnesus. It saved time and money, not to mention lives. Today, ships can pass through the canal that traverses the narrowest part of the Isthmus of Corinth, but in Phoebe's lifetime, no canal existed. Instead, this ingenious alternative, the Diolkos, saved a long boat trip around the Peloponnesian Peninsula; the southernmost tip of the peninsula, known as Cape Maleae, was, as Strabo testified, an especially dangerous part of the journey, and many lives were lost in the effort to sail past Maleae.

Although the exact date of the construction of the Diolkos is unknown, Thucydides, the author of the *History of the Peloponnesian War* (431 BC), knew of it as an already ancient structure. Many attribute its construction to Periander, ruler of Corinth from 627–587 BC. One thing that is certain is that the Diolkos was an invaluable means of transporting goods from the Saronic Gulf to the Corinthian Gulf by land so that they could then be sent on by ship to other regions. Moreover, it was an important source of revenue for Corinth because, like many modern roadways, there was a fee for its use.

While using the Diolkos was much safer than sailing around the peninsula, dragging boats and cargo over it was backbreaking and expensive work. It is no surprise, then, that efforts were made more than once to dig a canal through the Isthmus of Corinth. One was begun by Periander, but not completed.[25] Subsequent unsuccessful attempts were made by Demetrius Poliorcetes, king of Macedonia (294–288 BC) who sought passage for his fleets, and again by Julius Caesar, Caligula, and Nero. It was only in 1893, however, that the Corinth Canal (6,343 meters long and 25 meters wide) was finally realized after more than a decade of construction and great expense.

The Sanctuaries in Kenchreai

Kenchreai was accorded fame by Lucius Apuleius of Madauros (ca. AD 123–170), author of *Metamorphoses* (known also as *The Golden Ass*). The story is about a man named Lucius whose curiosity and desire to perform magic leads to a long and bitter journey. Lucius casts a spell, intending to transform himself into a bird; instead, he is accidentally transformed into an ass. For much of the book, Lucius, in the form of an ass, narrowly escapes one disaster after another. At the end of the tenth and penultimate book of *Metamorphoses*, the unfortunate Lucius, still in the form of an ass, escapes to Kenchreai where he is finally able to rest in peace for a while:

I stole secretly out of the gate that was next to me, and ran away with all my force. After about six miles I very swiftly passed to Cenchreae which is the most famous town of all the Corinthians, bordering on the seas called Aegean and Saronic. There is a great and mighty haven frequented with the ships of many a sundry nation, and there because I would avoid the multitude of people, I went to a secret place of the seacoast . . . where I laid me down upon the bosom of the sand to ease and refresh myself; for now the day was past and now the chariot of the sun gone down, and I lying in this sort on the ground did fall in a sweet and sound sleep. (Apuleius, *Metamorphoses*, 10.35)[26]

As book 11 opens, Lucius is wakened from his deep sleep. He prays to Isis, begging to be restored to human form. In an altered state of consciousness, Lucius encounters the goddess who promises to answer his prayer (*Metamorphoses*, 11.5-6).[27] The promised transformation occurs during a lavish procession in honor of Isis (11.13), which is described in some detail. Placement of this event in Kenchreai and his flattering description of the bustling port city suggest that Apuleius thought highly of Kenchreai, perhaps because it was an important center for the worship of Isis, or perhaps because he had a significant experience of the goddess there.[28]

The existence of a sanctuary in Kenchreai dedicated to Isis (and another to Asklepios) is also mentioned by the second-century Greek traveler and author Pausanias whose *Description of Greece* was a guidebook for pilgrims:

The names of the Corinthian harbors were given them by Leches and Cenchrias, said to be the children of Poseidon and Peirene the daughter of Acheloüs, though in the poem called *The Great Eoeae* Peirene is said to be a daughter of Oebalus. In Lechaeum are a sanctuary and a bronze image of Poseidon and on the road leading from the Isthmus to Cenchreae a temple and ancient wooden image of Artemis. In Cenchreae are a temple and a stone statue of Aphrodite. After it, on the mole running into the sea, a bronze image of

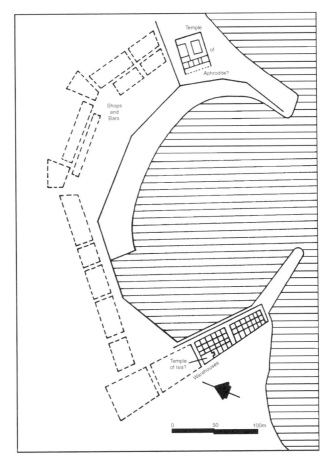

Figure 3: Harbor at Kenchreai

Poseidon, and at the other end of the harbor sanctuaries of
Asklepios and of Isis. (Pausanias, *Description of Greece*, 2.3)[29]

Pausanias states that the harbor at Kenchreai was named after
Kenchrias, the son of Poseidon and Peirene and that one could
see a bronze statue of Poseidon on a mole (breakwater) located
at the southern end of the harbor. Pausanias identifies two temples

at the south end of the harbor front, one dedicated to Isis, the ancient goddess of the Nile, and the other to Asklepios, the popular Greek god of healing. There was also a temple of Aphrodite located on the north side of the harbor front. While some archaeologists believe that remains of these sanctuaries have been located, debate on these matters is lively.

Remains of the breakwater and the warehouses that once stood at the southern end of the ancient port are still visible. Near the breakwater are the remnants of fish tanks that were used for storage. A large, well-preserved brick building, built in the latter part of the first century AD and extended in the fourth century when it was joined to another, is located at the northeast end of the harbor. The resulting structure consisted of several courts, a stoa (an open colonnade with a back wall to which columns were joined by the roof), and a peristyle (a courtyard with a covered walkway all the way around it, with columns holding up the ceiling so you can see out into the garden) on which faced enclosed rooms. There is no agreement on the identity of this complex. For some, it is the sanctuary of Aphrodite,[30] while others posit a Roman villa.[31]

Robert Scranton claims, somewhat tentatively, to have found evidence of sanctuaries of Asklepios and Isis at the southwest end of Kenchreai's harbor.[32] If he is correct, the Isis sanctuary was located behind the warehouses along the southwest pier. Built in approximately AD 100, it included a fountain court complex, with the temple and the hall behind. Moreover, a spectacular find of glass panels that depict Egyptian characteristics and motifs also discovered at this site may have been destined for the Isis sanctuary.[33] Here again, however, there is no consensus regarding the identification of these remains. Richard M. Rothaus, for example, believes that the fountain court and entrance hall may represent a Nymphaeum (a monument consecrated to the nymphs) and the temple of Isis, he insists, has not been found.[34] While archaeologists continue to scrutinize the evidence, one thing is clear: Pausanias's description of the statues, the temple, and the sanctuaries suggest that Aphrodite, Poseidon, Asklepios, and Isis were important deities for the residents of Kenchreai.

There is also archaeological evidence of Christian occupation in Kenchreai, but such evidence certainly postdates Phoebe. Excavations in the summers of 1963 and 1964 revealed the remains of a Christian basilica built over the remains of Roman warehouses.[35] This early sixth-century church contained an apse, a single nave, columns, and capitals, and was decorated with fine mosaics and frescoes. It was used until the early seventh century when it was destroyed by fire.[36] Phoebe did not worship in such a magnificent structure. In major cities such as Rome and Alexandria, Judeans[37] worshiped in large buildings known as *prosuchai*, while Christ-believers gathered in houses owned or rented by members of the Jesus movement.[38] The same was true in Kenchreai. Jesus groups probably met in various kinds of houses owned by members such as Phoebe, no doubt within earshot of a variety of cultic practices. There is as yet no archeological evidence of these meeting places, however.

The Jesus Group in Kenchreai

Archaeology reveals a great deal about ancient Kenchreai, but so far tells us little about Christ-believers in that town. Nevertheless, we can glean information from the New Testament about how the gospel came to Kenchreai. During Phoebe's lifetime, both Corinth and Kenchreai were located in the Roman province of Achaia. Paul's first letter to the Corinthians was addressed to "the church of God which is at Corinth, to those sanctified in Christ Jesus, called to be saints together with all those who in every place call on the name of our Lord Jesus Christ, both their Lord and ours" (1 Cor 1:2). This letter is intended not only for Jesus groups in Corinth but for the entire Jesus movement. Moreover, given the proximity of Corinth and Kenchreai and the strong commercial ties between them, there is little doubt that this letter found its way to Kenchreai. Furthermore, the second letter to the Corinthians, while addressed to Jesus groups in Corinth, was also destined for "all the saints who are in the whole of Achaia" (2 Cor 1:1), and Kenchreai was situated in the Roman province of Achaia. In this letter, Paul tells the intended audience that he, Timothy, and Silvanus have been commissioned by God to preach the gospel among them (2 Cor 1:19-22). Given the letter's destination ("the whole of Achaia"), it seems that Kenchreai was one of their success stories. Without a doubt, then, Phoebe and Paul were well acquainted.

A reference in a fifth-century commentary on the letters of Paul by Theodoret, bishop of Cyrus, provides some insight into the size and operations of the Jesus group in Kenchreai: "Cenchreae is the largest town in Corinth, so the impact of the preaching there calls for admiration. In a short time it filled with piety not only the cities but also the towns. And so large was the congregation of the church of Cenchreae that it even had a woman deacon, one both famous and celebrated. She had so great a wealth of virtuous actions as to earn such encomiums from the apostolic tongue" (Theodoret, *Commentary on the Fourteen Epistles of the Holy Apostle Paul: The Letter to the Romans: Chapter 16:1-2*).[39] If Theodoret is correct, the Jesus group in Kenchreai was active and influential in spreading the gospel throughout the Corinthia where at least thirty-seven towns or forts were known to have existed.[40] The picture we are left with is one of a large, well-established Jesus group in the busy, bustling port of Kenchreai, from whose ranks representatives brought the good news to other towns and cities in the Corinthia. Phoebe, a female *diakonos* in this assembly (Rom 16:1) whose virtuous actions had earned her an honorable public reputation, was an associate of Paul, laboring to spread the gospel of Jesus Christ throughout Achaia.

CHAPTER 3

Phoebe, a Deacon

Saint Paul introduces Phoebe as *diakonos* (Rom 16:1). Exactly what he means by this term is somewhat problematic. While in English usage the title "deaconess" designates female deacons, the Greek noun *diakonos* is masculine and has no feminine form in the New Testament. English translations of the Greek New Testament render the word *diakonos* into English in a number of ways. Some versions offer an English equivalent, others simply transliterate (that is, they write the Greek word in Roman characters). As a rule, transliteration (for example, "baptism," "apostle," "Christ") indicates that the translators could not find an equivalent word in the receptor language. In the case of *diakonos*, the Revised Standard Version (RSV), for example, employs the words "servant" (Rom 13:4; 15:8), "agent" (Gal 2:17), "minister" (Eph 3:7; 6:21; Col 4:7; 1 Tim 4:6), and the transliterations "deacon" (Phil 1:1; 1 Tim 3:8, 12, 13) and "deaconess" (Rom 16:1). Moreover, comparison of English translations of a single New Testament verse containing the word *diakonos* reveals a number of variants. Consider Romans 16:1. Here, the King James Version, the New King James Version, the New International Version, and the New American

Standard Version all employ the word "servant" for *diakonos*. For the same verse, other translations use the words "leader" (Contemporary English Version), "minister" (New American Bible), "deaconess" (RSV; New Jerusalem Bible), and "deacon" (New Revised Standard Version). Obviously, translators are motivated by different factors and, in this case, their choices impact how readers of English Bibles understand Phoebe's role in the assembly at Kenchreai. Does any one of these choices accurately reflect how Paul and his first-century contemporaries would have understood the word *diakonos*? If not, what word would best describe Phoebe's role?

Since meanings come from social systems and their institutions, perhaps it may be useful to search for the significance of a female *diakonos* in the early "deaconess" groups that revered Phoebe's memory. I therefore begin with a brief overview of diaconal ministry from the fourth to the nineteenth century, and here I am indebted to the comprehensive work of Jeannine Olson.[1] This synopsis is important because, as we shall see, the shape of diaconal ministry in many contemporary Christian denominations has been heavily influenced by events that began to shape the contours of the church as early as the fourth century. These things considered, we are better equipped to look again at Phoebe, especially at commendations by Origen and Chrysostom that convey the esteem in which she was held by the early church. Finally, I will move backward in time to probe the role of the *diakonos* in the first century AD and compare it with what we have seen in the fourth to twenty-first centuries. Our fundamental goal is to discover whether the word "deacon" means the same to us today as *diakonos* did to Phoebe, Paul, and their contemporaries. Only then can we discover a social context that enables us to translate *diakonos* in Romans 16:1 in a way that respects the cultural world of Phoebe.

Deaconesses in the Early Church

Ordained female deacons, referred to as deaconesses, were never numerous in the western Roman Empire. In fact, the Council of Orange (AD 441) and the Council of Orleans (AD 533) expressly forbade the ordination of deaconesses.[2] The attitude was different in the Orthodox Church where, from the third to the twelfth centuries, ordained deaconesses were numerous. For reasons unknown, however, their presence gradually faded, even though there was no official decree to eliminate them. Today there is lively discussion and much hope in some Orthodox circles that the office of ordained deaconess will be rejuvenated.

There are two early Middle Eastern documents that provide insight into the role of deaconesses at this time: the third-century *Didascalia Apostolorum* and the fourth-century *Apostolic Constitutions*.[3] The *Didascalia Apostolorum*, or *Teaching of the Apostles* (AD 220–250), records that both deacons and deaconesses were appointed by the bishop: "Wherefore, O bishop, appoint thee workers of righteousness as helpers who may cooperate with thee unto salvation. Those that please thee out of all the people thou shalt choose and appoint as deacons; a man for the performance of the most things that are required, but a woman for the ministry of women" (*Didascalia* 3.12).[4] According to the *Apostolic Constitutions* (ca. AD 380), deacons received men who had been baptized and deaconesses received the women. Moreover, these sources reveal that the ordination of deaconesses reflected that of other clergy. They were ordained at the altar by the bishop during a eucharistic liturgy at the same point in the service when male deacons were ordained.[5] Moreover, they received Communion with the other clergy. Although the liturgical role of the deacon was more extensive than that of the deaconess, it is clear that deaconesses were members of the clergy.

Constantine's adoption of Jesus-group beliefs and behaviors and his subsequent formation of Christianity as a political religion in the fourth century caused its ranks to swell. Given the gendered division of labor in the institutionalized political religion, the growing numbers of adult women requiring baptism contributed to the need for more deaconesses to minister to female initiates. Deaconesses performed a variety of services for Christian congregations, especially for female members. They assisted their bishops in the instruction and baptism of women. They acted as doorkeepers responsible for keeping order and finding places for female members of the congregation. They taught doctrine, visited and brought Communion to women who were sick, distributed alms, provided food and shelter for the poor, offered hospitality to travelers, and even founded monastic communities[6] whose members ministered to the hungry and the sick.

In the *Didascalia*, deaconesses are likened to the women who supported Jesus and the Twelve by providing for them out of their own means: "For this cause we say that the ministry of a deaconess is especially needful and important. For our Lord and Savior also was ministered unto by women ministers: Mary Magdalene; Mary, the daughter of James and the mother of Jose; and the mother of the sons of Zebedee, with other women besides."[7] This is an important comparison for two reasons. First, it suggests that deaconesses could act as patrons, a topic that will be addressed in chapter 4. Second, this parallel orients the ministry of the deaconess to Christ: she serves him.

The earliest extant prayer for the ordination of deaconesses is found in the *Apostolic Constitutions*:

> O Eternal God, the Father of Our Lord Jesus Christ, the creator of man and woman, who did replenish with the Spirit Miriam (Exod 15:20-21), Deborah (Judg 4–5), Anna (Luke 2:36), and Huldah (2 Kgs 22:14-20); who did not disdain that your only-begotten Son should be born of woman; who also in the tabernacle of the testimony and in the temple, did ordain women to be keepers of your holy gates; look down now upon this your servant, who is ordained for the diaconate, and grant her your Holy Spirit. Cleanse her from all that can defile flesh or spirit, so that she may worthily accomplish the work which is committed to her

to your glory and the praise of your Christ, with whom glory and adoration be to you, and the Holy Spirit forever. Amen. (*Apostolic Constitutions* 8.3.20)[8]

This prayer affirms the dignity of women, their receptivity to God's Spirit, and their participation in the prophetic ministry. Moreover, it implies that the ordination of the deaconess originates with God. She participates in God's mission and, by the grace of the Holy Spirit, her ministry will bear fruit.

The prayers for the ordination of deaconesses used by the Church of Constantinople survive in eighth-century manuscripts. The second ordination prayer gives special recognition to Phoebe:

> Sovereign Lord, you who do not reject women offering themselves and desiring to minister in your holy houses, in accordance with what is fitting, but rather receive them into an order of ministers, bestow the grace of your Holy Spirit also upon this your servant who desires to offer herself to you, and fill her with the grace of the diaconate, just as you gave the grace of your diaconate to Phoebe, whom you called to the work of ministry. O God, grant that she may persevere blamelessly in your holy temples, to cultivate appropriate conduct, especially prudence, and make your servant perfect so that she, standing at the judgment seat of your Christ, may receive the worthy reward of her good conduct. Through the mercy and love for humanity of your only begotten Son, with whom you are blessed, together with your all-holy, good and life-giving Spirit, now and ever and unto the ages of ages. Amen. (*The Byzantine Ordination Rite of the Deaconess*)[9]

The prayer begins with a strong affirmation of God's acceptance of women called to serve as deaconesses, perhaps reflecting opposition to the ordination of deaconesses in some regions. The divine origin of Phoebe's role as *diakonos* is claimed for the ordinand, and even though the church was separated from the historical Phoebe by at least three centuries, she was not forgotten. Indeed, Phoebe is celebrated here as a prototype for the ordained deaconess.

From Constantine to Luther

The fourth century brought changes that influenced the role of the clergy. As noted, the pre-Constantinian Jesus groups were transformed into political-religious Christian churches that grew under the protection and patronage of Emperor Constantine (AD 306–337). As church ranks swelled, it became necessary for bishops to delegate more responsibility to other clerics. As a result, the roles of presbyter and deacon quickly evolved. While presbyters became more closely aligned with congregations and administration of the Eucharist, the duties of fourth-century deacons included property management and administration of monetary gifts to the church. In the fifth to seventh centuries, as the wealth of the church grew in properties and material resources, the administrative duties of deacons became more complex. Furthermore, as time passed, more and more responsibility for the care of the poor was placed on the church by the Roman Empire. Bishops called upon deacons and deaconesses to meet the growing needs.

As Christian congregations grew between the fourth and seventh centuries, the liturgical role of the deacon also grew. Deacons assumed responsibility for the proclamation of the gospel. They blessed the paschal candle at the Easter Vigil, acted as cantors, announced the various parts of the liturgy, dismissed catechumens before the Eucharist, distributed the cup, announced the names of those who had made donations to the church, and dismissed the congregation. Deacons received Communion after bishops and presbyters, a practice that symbolized the importance of their role in the church.

Despite the deacon's important role, however, the Council of Nicea (AD 325) declared them as a lower status, below that of presbyters, and forbade them to sit with presbyters. Moreover, in the late fourth or early fifth century, a complex order of offices was beginning to manifest itself in the Western church. The growing need for presbyters led to the preparation of men for ordained ministry in the church. Under the watchful eye of the bishop, men passed through eight grades of clergy: doorkeeper, lector, exorcist, acolyte, subdeacon, deacon, presbyter, and bishop. As a result, the role of the permanent deacon began to wane. Although deacons still exercised liturgical functions and engaged in ministry to the poor, presbyters and stewards began to usurp their responsibility for property management and social ministry. In time, the diaconate would be no more than a stepping stone toward priesthood.

The fourth century also saw the beginning of a movement toward mandatory celibacy for clerics in certain geographical regions. At the time of the Council in Ancyra (AD 314), a deacon was only permitted to marry if he had made his intentions to marry known to his bishop before ordination; deaconesses were required to adopt celibacy. In the western Roman Empire, couples were expected to separate when the husband became a presbyter or bishop, while, in the eastern Roman Empire, only bishops were obliged to separate from their wives. Despite the directives, clergy were slow to adopt a celibate lifestyle. The Second Lateran Council (AD 1139) pronounced the marriages of subdeacons, deacons, and priests null and void. In defiance of the declaration, until the Protestant Reformation, many continued to live with their wives and have families.

After the fall of Rome (AD 476), the church inherited greater responsibility for care and education of the poor, with monastic communities playing a leading role in the ministry of hospitality. By the seventh century, there were "deaconries" in Rome, centers staffed by monks who distributed food to the poor and cared for them, tasks that had long been the responsibility of deacons. In the Middle Ages, the number of monastic communities of women and men increased, and their response to the social needs of the time formed an integral part of their vocation. By the thirteenth century, however, many monastic communities were less directly involved with the poor, their needs now being met by newly founded apostolic communities such as the Dominicans, Franciscans, and Poor Clares, communities dedicated to preaching, teaching, and serving the poor, especially in urban areas. Gone were the days when deacons were the primary agents of social outreach. In fact, during the late Middle Ages and the Renaissance, secular governments and agencies began to assume control of relief for the poor, eventually dominating what was once a major element of diaconal ministry. The diaconate was now a stage in priestly formation and the role of the deacon was primarily liturgical. For their part, deaconesses had all but disappeared.

The Reformation

Some sixteenth-century Protestant reformers desired to bring back the model of diaconal ministry, which they believed to have been the norm in emerging Christianity. Their perception of the deacon, based on their understanding of Acts 6:1-6, was primarily of one who brought relief to the poor on behalf of the church. Martin Luther and others believed that the apostles appointed the seven men (Acts 6:3) to see that Hellenist widows were not overlooked in the distribution of food. The work of the seven freed the apostles to preach the gospel. This interpretation of the Acts passage led Luther to argue that the real role of the deacon was to be the church's minister to the poor. While Luther's vision of the diaconate was not adopted by all Lutheran congregations, in some cases, lay individuals called deacons administered the so-called poor chest, a store of funds donated by members of the church and used by deacons to purchase and distribute aid to the poor.

John Calvin had more success in reviving the vision of the deacon as an angel of mercy. For Calvin, the primary responsibility of deacons was to care for the sick and the poor; they were also to administer the funds that would enable them to do so.

In the church constitutions that he wrote for the city of Geneva (AD 541), Calvin included four orders of office: pastors, doctors, elders, and deacons. He promoted the laying on of hands for deacons to symbolize their dedication to God. In time, this four-part division became a model for other Reformation churches throughout the world. Calvin also encouraged women to devote themselves to the needs of the poor and looked to Phoebe (Rom 16:1-2) as a model for female deacons and widows.

Certain sects were more likely to have deaconesses than others. In the case of Anabaptists who practiced adult baptism, deacons and, in some places, deaconesses assisted in baptismal ceremonies. They also helped to meet the needs of the poor in their communities. Some congregations held their goods in common so that the needs of all members would be met. Hutterite communities, which developed out of the Anabaptist movement, had two types of ordained deacons: those who preached and those who administered the community's finances. Within the Anabaptist movement, deaconesses gained considerable importance and contributed to the rise of the deaconess movement in the nineteenth and twentieth centuries.

Protestant denominations looked to the "plain sense" of Scripture and to their shared images of nascent Christianity for their understanding of diaconal ministry, which they believed to have consisted primarily of the duty to care for the poor. In Roman Catholicism, however, the diaconate emerged from the Council of Trent (AD 1545–1563) as basically a stepping stone to the priesthood. Much of the ministry to the sick and to the poor among Roman Catholics was provided not by deacons but by numerous religious communities established in the sixteenth century, including a number of congregations of vowed women religious.

The Seventeenth to Twentieth Centuries

At this time, the Roman Catholic diaconate was a phase in priestly formation and diaconal service was mainly liturgical.

In Protestant circles, the social works of deacons gradually passed into the hands of the state. In some places, however, deacons of Reformed churches continued to administer finances and serve the poor.

As the Reformed Church spread into France and into modern-day Belgium and the Netherlands, the diaconate went with it. The diaconate possessed a diverse profile in the French reformed tradition. In some places, deacons were even permitted to preach and to teach the faithful, while women performed diaconal service, particularly in larger centers where they served as nurses for other women, cared for the poor, and assisted with the collection and distribution of alms. Diaconal ministry also found its way to Scotland and England. In Scottish Presbyterianism, male deacons formed part of the local governing body of the church and assisted in the distribution of alms to the poor. In England, the Westminster Assembly (AD 1643) promoted service to the poor as the primary focus of deacons.

Lutheran and Baptist Churches brought diaconal ministry to some parts of North America. Lutheran Churches employed lay and ordained deacons. Lay deacons had both liturgical and administrative functions, often representing the congregation at annual conventions. While lay deacons remained deacons, ordained deacons were destined to become pastors. In the First Baptist congregations of New England, deacons looked after church finances and the community's material resources. Widows engaged in ministries typical of the deaconess: visiting the sick and assisting the poor.

In many ways, the deaconess movement had tremendous appeal to nineteenth- and early twentieth-century women, especially in Europe, in part because of the scarcity of vocational options for women, but also because it offered an experience of community and security in old age. Their role and that of deacons was very much like Luther's vision of individuals engaged in social welfare and committed to meeting the needs of the poor. Germany's Inner Mission trained men and women to work in prisons, hospitals, schools, hostels, poorhouses, halfway houses, and many other institutions established to meet the social needs of the time. European deaconesses often trained and served as nurses, and their ministry spread rapidly to other areas of Europe, the Middle East, and North Africa. The deaconess movement was not as widespread in England as in Europe because communities of vowed religious women performed the same tasks. Nevertheless, deaconesses gained a foothold in some dioceses where they were commissioned by the bishop to do parish work. By the mid-twentieth century, the Church of England was ordaining deaconesses. There were Methodist deaconesses as well who served as nurses, teachers, home visitors, and even preachers. In the United States and Canada, large numbers of congregations of vowed religious women performed the tasks of deaconesses, thereby limiting the need for and number of deaconesses in many parts of these countries.

The Diaconate Today

Olson's work has demonstrated that diaconal ministry has had a long and varied history in some Christian traditions. Over the centuries, the numbers of ordained deacons and deaconesses greatly declined in many places, but diaconal ministry did not go away completely. Today, it is finding a new face in some churches, and the numbers of permanent deacons and deaconesses are on the rise, particularly in the Anglican, Lutheran, Methodist, and Roman Catholic traditions. The New Testament plays an important role in how these individuals understand their vocation and ministry.

The office of deaconess has existed in the United Methodist Church since 1888. There were male diaconal ministers until 1996, when the General Conference decided to withdraw that ministerial option. In 2004, however, the Office of Home Missioner was established as a new vocational option for laymen. Today, the Offices of Deaconess and Home Missioner are full-time vocations in the United Methodist Church. This community of deaconesses and home missioners is rooted in Scripture and strongly committed to God's mission of justice and service. Its ministry to the poor is ecumenical and global in its outreach.[10] While the primary focus of its members is service in the world, they also serve as musicians, liturgists, educators, and business administrators. Furthermore, they assist elders as they preside over the sacraments of baptism and Holy Communion, conduct marriages, and oversee funerals.

In response to increasing social needs, some Lutheran Churches reintroduced deacons in the mid-nineteenth century. Today they are recognized and hold office in a number of places. Deacons in the Evangelical Lutheran Church (New York and Delaware-Maryland synods) engage in liturgical and pastoral ministry.[11] An Association of Lutheran Deaconesses, in place since 1919, oversees the theological education and formation of laywomen for service to the church and the world.[12] Their ministries include congregational work, church administration, hospice, prison ministry, spiritual direction, overseas missions, and social services. Jesus' command that his disciples wash one another's feet (John 13:14) is an integral part of how they understand their ministry of love and service to the poor and marginalized.

In the Anglican tradition, men and women are ordained as deacons before they are ordained as priests. This is known as the transitional diaconate. There is also, however, an option to become a vocational deacon, that is to say, a permanent deacon. The North American Association for the Diaconate exists to support Anglican deacons who are called to liturgical ministry, including proclamation of the word, to the training of laity for various roles, but especially to the ministry of social justice.[13] Vocational deacons are strongly encouraged to serve among the sick, the poor, and the oppressed.

Similarly, ordination to the transitional diaconate, normally for one year, is part of the formation process for Roman Catholic men aspiring to serve as priests. In 1967, Roman Catholic bishops reinstated the office of permanent deacon. This meant that Roman Catholic laymen, married or single, now had the option of ordination to the diaconate. Permanent deacons share in the ministry of the bishop by assisting with liturgical and sacramental services to Roman Catholic laity, especially in areas where there are few or no priests.[14] They, too, see ministry to the poor as an integral part of their call. Today, permanent deacons serve in over a hundred countries, the majority found in the United States, Canada, Italy, Germany, and Brazil.

The United Church of Canada (UCC) was formed in 1925 by the merger of the Methodist, Presbyterian, and Congregational Churches.[15] Before union, the Methodist and Presbyterian Churches had deaconesses while the Congregational Church did not.[16] The two deaconess groups soon amalgamated. In 1936, women in the UCC were admitted to ordained ministry, yet few deaconesses chose ordained ministry. During the Second World War, the decline in numbers of male ministers paved the way for deaconesses to serve as lay supply ministers who functioned as ordained ministers. In 1948, the UCC began to contemplate the possibility of making the diaconate an order of ministry, open to both men and women. Today's UCC diaconal ministers play a unique role in the UCC. They are commissioned to carry out a ministry of education, social outreach, and pastoral care.[17] Members of the one Order of Ministry in the United Church of Canada, they share fully with those who are ordained. With permission from the United Church Conference, diaconal ministers may be engaged to baptize and preside at communion like their ordained counter-parts. A major aspect of their vocation is to bring people together to work for universal justice, healing, and dignity.

Although each of the Christian traditions mentioned briefly here has its unique understanding of the identity and role of the deacon or deaconess, service to the poor and dispossessed is an integral aspect of the vocation. Deacons today perform liturgical roles that include proclaiming the Word of God and preaching, but many perceive that service to the poor constitutes the essence of their call. Motivated by compassion for the dispossessed, they look to New Testament passages that speak of ministry to understand their identity and mission.

The contemporary diaconal context raises questions pertinent to our quest to understand Phoebe as *diakonos*. Does Christian diaconal ministry, as outlined in this brief overview of the fourth to twenty-first centuries, shed light on Phoebe's role as *diakonos* (Rom 16:1)? What did the role of *diakonos* consist of in first-century Jesus groups? How can we interpret New Testament passages that use the word *diakonos* or its cognates in a way that takes into consideration the vast differences between contemporary North American culture and the cultural world of first-century Mediterranean societies? Our aim in this chapter is to see how Phoebe's role as *diakonos* in a gender-separated world compares with that of deacons and deaconesses in ensuing centuries. We have seen that throughout the centuries, diaconal ministry was, in large part, a response to the needs of the poor.

Now it is time to move back into Phoebe's world to probe the role of *diakonos* in her time. As a prelude, we look briefly at how two early Christian writers remembered Phoebe.

Origen

We begin with Origen. Born of an Israelite mother in Alexandria, Egypt, in AD 185, Origen moved to Caesarea in Palestine in AD 232, where he founded a school. A prolific writer, Origen wrote books, homilies, letters, and numerous commentaries on Scripture. In the oldest extant commentary on Romans (ca. AD 246), he has the following to say about Romans 16:1-2:

> This passage teaches with apostolic authority that women are likewise appointed deacons of the church. With great praise and commendation Paul honors Phoebe, who was placed in this service in the church in Cenchreae, as he enumerates as well her illustrious accomplishments and says: She has assisted everyone to such an extent, that is, in her being at hand for necessities, that she even gave assistance to me in my necessities and apostolic labors with the complete dedication of mind. I would call her work similar to

the hospitality of Lot, who, while he received strangers at all times, one time even merited to receive angels in hospitality. In a similar way Abraham too, while he was always meeting strangers, merited even to have the Lord, together with angels, turn aside to his tent. So also this devout Phoebe—while she stood near everyone and served everyone—merited to assist and to serve the apostle as well. And therefore this passage teaches two things at the same time: As we have said, women are to be considered deacons in the church, and those who have assisted and who through good services have merited attaining unto apostolic praise ought to be received in the diaconate. He exhorts even this, that those who look after good works in the churches should receive, in turn, recompense and honor from the brothers, so that in whatever things there is a need, whether in spiritual or even fleshly services, they should be held in honor. (Origen, *Commentary on Romans* 10.17)[18]

Writing in a time when ordained deaconesses were actively serving the Christian church, Origen commences by stressing that the appointment of deaconesses in his own time and place was sanctioned by Paul, and therefore, by the apostles. Moreover, his comment that Phoebe was appointed to serve as *diakonos* in the Jesus group in Kenchreai suggests that, in Origen's mind, she exercised some kind of official capacity there. This does not mean that Origen thought Phoebe had been ordained like deaconesses in his day. More likely, he thought of her as delegated to perform a particular role or to accomplish certain tasks for her community in Kenchreai.

In the citation above, Origen portrays Phoebe's many accomplishments and her contributions to Paul's ministry as analogous to the hospitality of Lot and Abraham. Comparison with Abraham, whose commitment to hospitality was renowned in Israelite tradition, is no small honor. Among nomadic tribes, hospitality ensured the survival of travelers who might otherwise have died in hostile desert conditions. Even today, hospitality remains a core value in Mediterranean culture. Many contemporary North

Americans tend to associate hospitality with acts of kindness done on behalf of family members or for friends. The practice of hospitality in the world of the Bible, however, has never been associated with entertaining family and friends. Hospitality in biblical times was always about dealing with strangers— complete strangers. We see this in the meaning of the word itself. While the word for hospitality does not appear in the Old Testament, the New Testament employs the Greek word *philoxenia* to mean "hospitality" (Rom 12:13; 1 Tim 3:2; Titus 1:8; 1 Pet 4:9). Literally speaking, *philoxenia* means "love" (*philos*) of the "stranger" (*xenos*). That is what the Bible essentially means by hospitality. It entails a process of receiving people and changing them from strangers into guests by offering them shelter, protection, and the best food at one's disposal.[19] The good host also ensured that the stranger's animals were taken care of and provisions were provided for the subsequent journey.

The transformation of the visitor from stranger to guest was often acknowledged through the ritual of foot washing. Foot washing was a common practice in antiquity because cities were filthy and foot odor was inevitable for anyone walking through them. Feet were either washed by the guests themselves or by household slaves. To the strangers he encounters at the Oaks of Mamre, Abraham says, "Let a little water be brought, and wash your feet, and rest yourselves under the tree, while I fetch a morsel of bread, that you may refresh yourselves" (Gen 18:4-5). Abraham brings the food that has been prepared, and while the strangers eat, he stands under a nearby tree (Gen 18:8). Origen's reference to Phoebe standing near and serving everyone vividly recalls the actions of Abraham who, as Origen says, is always offering hospitality to strangers. Having enjoyed a sumptuous meal and time for rest, the strangers are sent on their way by Abraham, most likely with provisions for their journey. They strike out for Sodom where they meet Lot who invites them to wash their feet and to spend the night in his household (Gen 19:1-2). Again, a sumptuous meal is offered. Later that evening, the men of Sodom threaten to dishonor Lot's guests, and, like any honorable host, he attempts to protect them. The strangers' response is to offer information that will ensure the survival of both Abraham's and Lot's families. The childless Abraham and Sarah are promised a son (Gen 18:10). Lot is warned of the imminent destruction of Sodom and advised to immediately evacuate his family (Gen 19:12-13). Related to this is Origen's conclusion that those who, like Phoebe, have done good works ought to receive recompense and honor. Perhaps his most important point, however, is that Phoebe's service as *diakonos* in Kenchreai and her commendation by Paul lend strong support to the appointment of deaconesses to serve the churches in Origen's own time.

Chrysostom

Phoebe surfaces again in the writings of the great orator John Chrysostom, whose name means "golden-mouthed." Chrysostom was born in AD 347 in Antioch, Syria, ordained a priest in AD 386, and consecrated bishop of Constantinople in AD 398. His exegetical works include numerous homilies. In the section that precedes his homilies on Paul's letter to the Romans, Chrysostom heaps praises on Paul for his knowledge of the faith and his oratorical skills. In light of his great respect for Paul, Chrysostom's praise of Phoebe is high praise indeed.

Like Origen, Chrysostom was familiar with the office of deaconess. His friend Olympias was deaconess-abbess of a monastery of more than two hundred and fifty deaconesses and virgins that she founded in Constantinople prior to AD 398. His homily on Romans 15–16 has this to say about Phoebe:

> *I commend to you our sister Phoebe, a deacon of the church of Cenchreae.* See how many ways he takes to give her honor, for he has both mentioned her before all the rest, and called her sister. And it is no slight thing to be called a sister of Paul. Moreover, he has added her rank, by mentioning her being deacon.

Welcome her in the Lord as is fitting for the saints. That is, for the Lord's sake, that she may enjoy honor among you. For he that receives a person for the Lord's sake, even though it is not a great one that he receives, receives him with attention. But when it is a saint, consider what attention he ought to have shown him. And this is why he adds, *as is fitting for the saints*, as such persons ought to be received. For she has two grounds for her having attention shown her by you, both that of her being received for the Lord's sake, and that of her being a saint herself.

Help her in whatever she may require from you. You see how little he burdens them. For he does not say, "that you dispatch" but that you contribute your own part, and reach out a hand to her, and that in whatever business she has need. Do not offer her that which she does not need, but that which she requires of you. But she will ask in such things as lie in your power. Then again there comes a very great praise of her. *She has been a patron of many and of myself also.*

See his judgment. First comes the praises, then he entreats, and then again, he praises her, so placing on each side of the needs of this blessed woman her praises. How could this woman not be blessed, she who enjoyed such favorable testimony from Paul, she who could assist him with his mission to the whole world (*oikoumenē*)? For this was the summit of her good deeds, and so he placed it last, and so he says: *and of myself as well*. And to whom does, *and of myself as well* refer? This refers to the one who was the herald of the whole world (*oikoumenē*), he who suffered so much, of him who is equal to assisting tens of thousands. (Chrysostom, *Homilies on Romans* 30.2; emphasis in original)[20]

Chrysostom deems it important that Paul names Phoebe first in his list of greetings. In collectivistic societies, prominence implies honor. Paul's comments about Phoebe function as a letter of reference for her (Rom 16:1-2). As her referee, Paul is more intent on creating a favorable reception for Phoebe than he is on setting her above the recipients of the letter. He wants the Ephesians to treat her as an insider, that is, as one of them. That is why the first descriptor that Paul uses for Phoebe is "our sister." As a member of a Jesus group, she is his sister and theirs as well. Paul also describes Phoebe as one of "the saints," a name he often uses for Christ-believers (Rom 1:7; 1 Cor 1:2; 2 Cor 1:1; Phil 1:1). This too establishes common ground between Phoebe and the Ephesians. If Paul succeeds in convincing them that Phoebe is a trusted insider, they will extend the same loyalty and solidarity to her that they are expected to extend to one another, and they will help her in any way possible.

Chrysostom emphasizes that Paul praises Phoebe because she has been a patron to many people, including Paul himself. For Chrysostom, this is Phoebe's greatest accomplishment. He understands her patronage as some kind of assistance in Paul's task of bringing the good news to "the whole world." The Greek word that Chrysostom uses here is *oikoumenē*, which can mean "the inhabited earth" or "the world as an administrative unit," in other words, the Roman Empire. This latter sense is the better way to understand Chrysostom's comment. He would have known that Paul had brought the gospel to several centers within the Roman Empire. We will have much more to say about Phoebe's role as patron in the next chapter.

Diakonos in the New Testament

Phoebe is *diakonos* of an *ekklēsia* (a gathering of believers), a reference that seems to imply an official role for her among members of the Jesus group at Kenchreai (Rom 16:1). Was Phoebe like the deaconesses of Origen and Chrysostom's time, women who were ordained in large part to respond to the needs of women in Christian communities? Or did she function much like deacons and deaconesses do today? What was her role in the Jesus group in Kenchreai? To answer these questions, we will move back in time to see if first-century usage of *diakonos* and its cognates coheres with how diaconal ministry was understood and practiced in subsequent centuries. We will focus on *diakon-* words used in the New Testament: *diakonos* (usually translated as "deacon," "servant," or "minister"), *diakonein* (usually translated as "to serve"), and *diakonia* (usually translated as "ministry" or "service"). In this section, I draw heavily on two works by John Collins: his groundbreaking linguistic investigation of *diakon-* words in the New Testament and other Greek texts[21] and a book that he wrote for contemporary deacons.[22]

Acts 6:1-4

Contemporary diaconal ministers often turn to Acts 6:1-4 for inspiration: "Now in these days when the disciples were increasing in number, the Hellenists murmured against the Hebrews because their widows were neglected in the daily distribution [*diakonia*]. And the twelve summoned the body of the disciples and said, 'It is not right that we should give up preaching the word of God to serve [*diakonein*] tables. Therefore, brethren, pick out from among you seven men of good repute, full of the Spirit and of wisdom, whom we may appoint to this duty. But we will devote ourselves to prayer and to the ministry [*diakonia*] of the word.'" This rendition of the Greek suggests that the seven men to be appointed would be distributing food to widows who were not receiving their fair share. According to Collins, however, the notion of *diakonia* as "distribution" is incorrect; the abstract noun *diakonia* means to attend to people or to arrange for someone to attend to them.[23]

Collins' work is supported by Frederick Danker who defines *diakonia* as "service rendered in an intermediary capacity or mediation." Moreover, *diakonos* is "one who serves as an intermediary in a transaction, an agent, intermediary," that is, "one who gets things done at the behest of a superior, an assistant" and the verb *diakonein* means "to function as an intermediary" or "to act as a go-between or agent."[24] This means that the familiar translation "to serve tables" is misleading. Greek attendants did not wait on tables; they waited on the individuals who were at the tables. In fact, Collins concludes that the form of the

Greek word for "tables" used in Acts 6:2 indicates that, in this instance, *diakonein* involves the public and perhaps ritual fulfillment of responsibilities within the community. The Twelve, he argues, are talking about a duty that, like their own, is divinely commissioned. Collins offers a new reading of Acts 6:1-4:

> The Greek-speaking members of the community complained against those who spoke Aramaic that their housebound widows were being overlooked in the great preaching (*diakonia*) that was going on day by day in the environs of the Temple. So the Twelve summoned the whole complement of the disciples and said: "We cannot possibly break off our public proclamation before the huge crowds in the Temple to carry out a ministry (*diakonein*) in the households of these Greek-speaking widows. Brothers, you will have to choose seven men from your own ethnic group who are fully respected, empowered by the Spirit, and equipped for the task. We will then appoint them to the role that needs to be filled. That will mean that the Twelve can get on with attending to worship in the Temple and to our apostolic ministry (*diakonia*) of proclaiming the Word there."[25]

Collins' reading has much to commend it. Recall Luke's description of the Jesus group in Jerusalem. They shared their possessions with one another so that not a single member of the community was in need (Acts 4:32-35). The number of disciples was increasing because of the wondrous deeds performed by the apostles (4:15-16) in addition to their teaching and preaching (5:42–6:1). It is in this context of the preaching and healing ministry of the Twelve that we suddenly hear of the neglect of the widows (6:1). Moreover, immediately after the seven are appointed, Luke mentions how God's word has increased, suggesting that this increase has to do with the appointment of these men. In support of the association of the seven with the ministry of the Word rather than with the distribution of food are Luke's references to Stephen, who performed great signs and proclaimed the Word (6:8; 7:2-53), and Philip, who did likewise (8:5-8).

Mark 10:35-45

Diakon- words are also used in the New Testament to speak about service. One of the most famous of these is Jesus' teaching about why he has come: "But it shall not be so among you; but whoever would be great among you must be your servant [*diakonos*], and whoever would be first among you must be slave of all. For the Son of man also came not to be served [*diakonēthēnai*] but to serve [*diakonēsai*], and to give his life as a ransom for many" (Mark 10:43-45). Notice the *diakon* root in the last two Greek words. Each is a form of the verb *diakonein*: the first is passive (to be served) and the second is active (to serve).

To understand the nuances of the *diakon-* words in Mark 10:43-45, it is helpful to examine them in their gospel context. Jesus has been teaching his obtuse disciples about the fate that awaits him in Jerusalem: "Behold, we are going up to Jerusalem; and the Son of man will be delivered to the chief priests and the scribes, and they will condemn him to death, and deliver him to the Gentiles; and they will mock him, and spit upon him, and scourge him, and kill him; and after three days he will rise" (Mark 10:33-34). But no sooner has Jesus announced his impending death than the sons of Zebedee approach him to request that they sit, one at his right hand and one at his left in his "glory" (10:37). Their desire to acquire honor is understandable. They live in a world where all goods are thought to be in limited supply. Limited goods include not only material resources but intangible resources such as honor. If one person's honor increases, others perceive that their honor has decreased. Consequently, if the sons of Zebedee succeed in acquiring the two most prestigious places next to Jesus in his "glory" (honor), they will augment their honor while the other disciples will feel a loss of honor. In a society where honor is highly coveted, no one wants to lose it and everyone wants to gain it. Naturally, the other disciples become angry with James and John. There is not a disciple in the group who does not desire one of those prestigious places. The scene is one of competition and struggle, each desiring to increase his honor rating at the expense of the others. The struggle for honor, however, demonstrates a poignant lack of understanding about Jesus' identity and mission, and so he teaches them, this time about how they are to be in relationship with one another.

Disciples are not to be like foreign rulers and officials who exploit the masses to support their luxurious lifestyles while the exploited majority struggle daily to survive (Mark 10:42-43). In contrast to the elite minority whose interests are self-directed, relationships are to be highly valued in the community of disciples. They are not to compete with one another by striving to be first. On the contrary, the one who aspires to be great must become a servant (*diakonos*) and the one who desires to be first must be a slave (*doulos*) to everyone (10:43-44). They are to be motivated by generosity and not focus on what they will receive in return. By doing so, they will form a community of disciples bound closely together by ties of loyalty and affection. Notice the emphasis on the well-being of the group. Members are to sacrifice their own interests for the good of the group. The ideal ingroup in an honor-shame society is one where members do precisely that.

Jesus then tells them about how *he* will serve others. He will "give his life as a ransom for many" (Mark 10:45). In an honor-shame world, acting as a "ransom" does not mean exactly the same thing as it does in an individualistic setting. In first-century Mediterranean societies, one would be accepted as a ransom for others if one had a higher honor ranking than those being set free.[26] The higher the honor ranking of the captive, the higher the honor that the captors will gain. Mark identifies Jesus as the Son of God in the first verse of his gospel (Mark 1:1). This designation relegates a great deal of honor to Jesus. Jesus, however, will not just serve as a high-level captive. He will "give his life" so that others will be set free (10:45).

The existence of not one but three predictions of Jesus' passion and resurrection (Mark 8:31; 9:31; 10:33-34), indicates the significance of these events in the Gospel of Mark. When Peter rejects the idea that Jesus will suffer, he aligns himself with Satan whose function is to test whether individuals are loyal to God. Peter and those who, like him, cannot accept a suffering Messiah are not on God's side (8:33). Jesus strongly rejects their view, thereby revealing that he will remain steadfastly loyal to the mission of the God whom he has come to serve. In Mark's passion narrative, we learn that Jesus will freely accept the "cup" if that is what God wants of him (14:36). In the Bible, the term "cup" refers not only to a drinking vessel but also to "the limited and fixed amount of whatever God has to offer" individuals.[27] It symbolizes an individual's fate, in Jesus' case, his death and resurrection. The idea of baptism is related to this. In the New Testament, baptism is associated with the death and resurrection of Jesus; through baptism, believers share in the life brought by Jesus' death and resurrection (Rom 6:1-4). The sons of Zebedee unwittingly claim their readiness to accept the same "cup" and "baptism" as Jesus (Mark 10:39). But their eyes are fixed on acquiring honor while his eye is on the liberation of others through his death. The service that Jesus describes here is not akin to that of today's deacons and deaconesses. It is not about performing acts of charity motivated by compassion for the dispossessed. It is about fulfilling the commission given him by God to the point of giving his life, thereby demonstrating his abiding loyalty to God.

Luke 22:7-27

A related story about Jesus as *diakonos* occurs during the account of the Last Supper in Luke's gospel. Jesus and his disciples are now in Jerusalem, and he sends Peter and John to prepare the Passover meal (Luke 22:8). Jesus and his disciples gather in an upper room to celebrate the Passover. After sharing the second cup of wine with his disciples, Jesus reveals a shocking truth. The one who will hand him over to the political-religious authorities is reclining at the table with him. Jesus and his disciples are members of the same ingroup. Ideally, every one of them ought to be able to expect the utmost loyalty from every other member of the group. That one of Jesus' closest followers would share a meal with him, after having arranged to hand him over to outsiders (22:3-6), represents a horrendous breach of ingroup trust and solidarity. The disciples begin to argue with one another about the perpetrator's identity (22:23). This evolves into another dispute. This time they are vying for honor, arguing about which of them is the greatest (22:24). Jesus' response quickly overturns their concept of honor:

> And he said to them, "The kings of the Gentiles exercise lordship over them; and those in authority over them are called benefactors. But not so with you; rather let the greatest among you become as the youngest, and the leader as one who serves. For which is the greater, one who sits at table, or *one who serves* [*ho diakonōn*]? Is it not the one who sits at table? But I am among you as one who serves." (Luke 22:25-27; emphasis mine)

Jesus immediately sets them straight about how they are to relate to one another. The greatest is the one who becomes like the youngest. The disciples know well that honor increases with age; the youngest always has much less honor than the eldest. They also know what Jesus means when he asks who is greater, the one who reclines at table or the one who serves. The one at table is clearly the greater. Yet Jesus, their leader, is "like one who serves." Notice that Jesus *likens* himself to the one who serves. He is not saying that he *is* a waiter. What he is saying is that he does not grasp for honor. He chooses the lower place, thereby demonstrating his humility. His disciples are to do likewise.

Think of this passage in relation to the seven who are appointed by the apostles to assist with the needs of Hellenist widows (Acts 6:1-4). They are not appointed to distribute food to these women and their families. Rather, they are to pay attention to these women, to care for them by ensuring that they receive the Word of God. In this instance, *diakonein* is not about serving food but about teaching and preaching the gospel.[28]

Similarly here in Luke, Jesus is not saying that he has come to serve food. He is saying that true greatness is about choosing the lowest place.

Matthew 25:31-46

Another story that will illustrate the meaning of *diakon-* words in the New Testament is Matthew's judgment scene. Here, the Son of Man separates people into two groups, placing the sheep at his right hand and the goats at his left (Matt 25:32-33). Matthew's choice of the symbols of sheep and goat is deliberate. Earlier we described honor as a core cultural value in the Middle East. Honor is an individual's public claim to value that must be affirmed in the public sphere. The notion of shame goes hand in hand with honor. There are two kinds of shame: one is positive and one is negative. Negative shame is about being shamed or losing face in public. When that happens, one's entire family loses face. Positive shame, however, is about regard for one's honor. It is about doing whatever one needs to do to protect one's individual honor and, hence, that of one's family.

In traditional societies, animals often symbolize aspects of human society. In Mediterranean societies, sheep symbolize honor and are associated with men; men take care of them. Goats symbolize shame and are associated with women who care for them.[29] Matthew's judgment scene places the sheep on the right side, the side associated with honor, and the goats on the left, the side associated with shame. Judgment in this scene has to do with whether or not hospitality had been offered to strangers. It was men who usually performed the role of host, thereby extending hospitality to strangers on behalf of their households. In the parable, those who have acted hospitably have acted honorably by extending hospitality to those in need of it. They are depicted as sheep, animals associated with the core cultural value of honor. Matthew then depicts those who have acted shamefully by their failure to extend hospitality as goats, animals associated with the core value of shame. Matthew's choice of sheep and goats to symbolize the two groups of people is not intended to denigrate women in any way. These animals are chosen because of their associations with honor and shame. The teaching in chapters 24 and 25 of Matthew is directed to Jesus' disciples. By means of these parables, Matthew is trying to teach the people for whom he authors his gospel, a community consisting of women and men, about the importance of hospitality. Both the *sheep* and the *goats* symbolize groups comprised of both men and women.

Passages such as Matthew's judgment scene inspire the modern vision of the permanent diaconate as ministry rooted in service to the needy. To feed the hungry, give water to the thirsty, extend hospitality to the stranger, clothe the naked, and visit those in prison is to "minister to" (*diakonein*) Jesus himself (Matt 25:44). Failure to do so is failure to serve him (25:45). But as Collins points out, there is nothing in this story that suggests that service to the needy is the special call of a chosen few whom we call deacons. The story is situated in a section of Matthew that consists of instructions and parables of Jesus directed at his disciples (24:1–25:46). He teaches them that the Son of Man will gather together "all the nations" (25:32) when he comes in his glory. "All the nations" (*panta ta ethnē*) refers to all of the members of the house of Israel no matter where they are living. Once gathered, all are judged by the Son of Man on the basis of how they have treated the needy. While today's diaconate is often identified with this kind of service (*diakonia*), Matthew is saying that hospitality is the duty of *every* Christian.

Diakon- as Emissary

So far we have seen that in the New Testament *diakon-* words denote different meanings: preaching and teaching, acting humbly, and extending hospitality to strangers. We have seen that the *diakonia* of Jesus is about giving his life so that others might be set free. These examples, however, are by no means exhaustive.

The root meaning of *diakon* is that of "go-between." *Diakon-*
words do not necessarily involve the idea of humble service and
never express the idea of serving others for reasons of benevolence. In fact, *diakon-* words do not imply benefit either to the
person authorizing the action or to its recipient but stand for an
action done in the name of another.[30] A first-century *diakonos*
often functioned as an assistant to community leaders or as an
itinerant officer who served as liaison between Jesus groups.[31]
For Paul, the *diakonos* was also one who preached the gospel
(2 Cor 11:7, 23), thereby serving as God's authoritative spokes-
person or God's emissary; this portrayal of the *diakonos* is preva-
lent in some Pauline passages (2 Cor 3:6; 5:18; 6:4). In these and
other instances, Paul talks about individuals and groups acting
as agents or representatives of another. As emissary, the *diakonos*
took on a mission for a delegating authority. As emissary, the
diakonos functioned something like an apostle (*apostolos*), "one
who is sent," or in other words, a messenger. In fact, in many
situations, the word "emissary" is the more appropriate translation for New Testament occurrences of *diakonos* than is "servant"
or "waiter." Such is the case with Phoebe. As bearer of Paul's
letter of recommendation, she went to Ephesus on behalf of the
Jesus group in Kenchreai; she was an emissary.

How did Phoebe get to be an emissary? In individualistic
societies, individuals themselves, experiencing what they believe
to be a call to serve as deacons and deaconesses, present themselves as candidates for the diaconate. While they do require
references, the incentive to pursue this role comes from the individual. A member of a collectivistic society would never act
in this way, especially if the new role means an increase of honor.
To do so would appear self-seeking and constitute shameful
behavior. Notice that in the New Testament, individuals are
delegated as emissaries. Paul, Barnabas, and some others are
appointed (*tassō*) by the Jesus group in Antioch to approach the
apostles and elders in Jerusalem about the question of whether
circumcision is necessary for males joining Jesus groups (Acts
15:1-2). The verb *tassō* means to assign someone to a particular

task or function. The gospels use the same word when Jesus sends his disciples forth to heal the sick, to preach about the imminence of the kingdom (Luke 10:9), and to bear good fruit as a sign of their discipleship (John 15:8, 16). Luke also states that Paul and the others are sent on their way to Jerusalem by the assembly (Acts 15:3). That is to say, they go with the support and approval of those in Antioch who have sent them.

Emissaries were esteemed by their senders. The elders and apostles in Jerusalem, for example, send "leading men" from among them to Antioch with an important letter bearing instructions for membership in the Jesus group (Acts 15:22-29). The contribution for the Jesus group in Jerusalem is delivered by members of the Corinthian community who *are accredited* by letter (1 Cor 16:3). The verb is *dokimazō* and means "to regard something as genuine or worthy on the basis of testing."[32] These people are clearly trusted by their senders. Timothy is sometimes sent ahead of Paul to assist with issues and problems facing Jesus groups (Phil 2:19-24). Paul sends Timothy because he is his closest associate.[33] Paul's high opinion of Timothy is reflected in the fact that they are cosenders of three letters: 1 Thessalonians, Philippians, and 2 Corinthians. Moreover, Paul relates to Timothy as a father to a son, a very close relationship indeed. Timothy is an excellent example of one chosen to act as emissary because the sender has tremendous trust in him.

What can be said about Phoebe as emissary? To begin with, Phoebe was chosen by the assembly in Kenchreai to act as emissary to Ephesus. To qualify as such, she must have been highly respected and trusted, a leading woman. Moreover, she must have been viewed as competent to represent their interests. According to Theodoret, Phoebe was well-known in the towns and cities of the Corinthia. Recall his words, cited earlier:

> Cenchreae is the largest town in Corinth, so the impact of the preaching there calls for admiration. In a short time it filled with piety not only the cities but also the towns. And so large was the congregation of the [*ekklēsia*] of Cenchreae

that it even had a woman [*diakonos*], one both famous and celebrated. She had so great a wealth of virtuous actions as to earn such encomiums from the apostolic tongue—*patron as she herself has been to many including myself*, he says, note. Now, by *patronage* I am inclined to think he refers to her hospitality and care, and he rewards her with multiple compliments. I mean, it is likely she received him into one house for a short time—namely, the period he spent in Corinth—whereas he introduced her to the world, and on all land and sea she became famous: not only the Romans and Hellenists knew of her but also all the barbarians. (Theodoret, *Commentary on the Fourteen Epistles of the Holy Apostle Paul: The Letter to the Romans: Chapter 16:1-2*; emphasis in original)[34]

Theodoret writes that the preaching in Kenchreai was so successful that great numbers became Christ-believers. The congregation in Kenchreai was large and probably consisted of several groups meeting in houses of wealthier members. In fact, there were so many followers that a woman *diakonos* was needed; that woman was Phoebe. It is in this context of successful preaching of the gospel that Theodoret refers to Phoebe as "famous and celebrated." She probably played a significant role in the spread of the gospel across the towns and cities of the Corinthia. In her cultural world, one can easily imagine that her role as *diakonos* sometimes involved ministry to women in the Jesus groups. But the fact that she took a letter of recommendation from Paul to the Ephesians suggests that her role was also one of emissary to other centers, and if she was as well known as Theodoret claims, Phoebe may have traveled much as representative of her community. Unfortunately, we do not know the precise nature of her mission to Ephesus. What we do know is that she was not involved in charitable work as we understand it today. Her role as *diakonos* did not stem from her personal feelings of compassion for the poor. She was called forth by her community to represent them in the spread of the gospel. Those whom Paul greets in Romans 16 have been intimately involved in this mission. Prisca and Aquila, in whose house Christ-believers meet, have risked their lives for Paul (Rom 16:3-5). The apostles Andronicus and Junia were imprisoned with Paul (16:7). Several others have labored faithfully to promote the gospel (16:6, 9, 12). Epaenetus was the first in Asia to become a follower of Christ (16:5), and Rufus is distinguished in the Lord (16:13). People such as these are well qualified to assist Phoebe with whatever her community may need. She was a *diakonos* who might need some assistance. But more than this, Paul asks the Ephesians to help her because she has been a *prostatis* (patron) of many people, including Paul himself (Rom 16:2). It is to this topic that we now turn.

CHAPTER 4

Phoebe, a Patron

Our portrait of Phoebe of Kenchreai is beginning to take shape. We know that as *diakonos*, a role best described as a "go-between," "agent," or "emissary," she played a significant role in the life of the Jesus group in the bustling port city of Kenchreai, throughout the Corinthia, and at least as far as Ephesus, which lay due east of Kenchreai across the Aegean Sea. While her role as *diakonos* accorded her honor within the Jesus group, it is not the sole indicator of Phoebe's honor rating. Of her Paul also uses the Greek noun *prostatis* (Rom 16:2), a word that does not occur elsewhere in the New Testament, and one that is subject to some debate as to its precise meaning.

Interestingly, in a ninth-century Arabic version of Paul's letter to the Romans, the latter part of 16:2 is rendered as "one in authority over [*prostatis*] many and over myself as well."[1] Thus, long ago, at least one translator depicted Phoebe as a woman who exercised authority over many. Not all contemporary translators follow suit, however. While some Bibles render *prostatis* as "benefactor" (New Revised Standard Version and New American Bible), a choice that accords Phoebe significant honor, others prefer less well-attested textual variants that describe her as "a helper" (Revised Standard Version), "a great help to" (New International Version), or one who "comes to the help of" (New Jerusalem Bible). The authors of scholarly commentaries and articles also part company when describing what *prostatis* means in terms of Phoebe's social role and activities. Some are convinced that *prostatis* denotes a person with considerable social status.[2] The fact that Paul introduces her as both *diakonos* and *prostatis* leads others to translate *prostatis* with an honorable title such as "leader" or "president"; a woman's leadership of the Jesus group in Kenchreai, it is thought, would suit a setting where Hellenized women served as priestesses.[3] Still others view Phoebe as a patron who assists the less fortunate and opens her home in Kenchreai to offer hospitality to strangers and to host meetings of Christ-believers.[4] The scope of Phoebe's influence and authority often enter into scholarly deliberations of her role in the life of the Jesus group. Fascinating questions arise. Was she, as some believe, more influential than Paul in the assembly at Kenchreai?[5] Did she have an authoritative role within and beyond the Jesus group in Kenchreai?[6] Or was she simply a woman of means who offered hospitality and practical help to many individuals?[7] Wherein does the truth about Phoebe of Kenchreai lie?

Simply stated, the title *prostatis* accorded to Phoebe by Paul implies prestige. It is the feminine form of the masculine term *prostatēs* ("ē" is pronounced like a long "a"). While *prostatēs* often refers to the sponsor of a private association and includes the notion of social protection provided by that sponsor, *prostatis* is attributed to patron-goddesses and means "protectress".[8] More generally speaking, *prostatēs* connotes "one who looks out for the interests of others, defender, guardian, benefactor" while *prostatis* refers to "a woman in a supportive role, a patron, or benefactor."[9] The feminine *prostatis* is one of several Latinisms that occur in the New Testament; in fact, it belongs to a group of Latinisms that signify Roman offices.[10] What do we mean by a Latinism?

The New Testament was written in a form of Greek that belongs to the large language family known as the Indo-European languages and includes most of the major languages of Europe and Asia. While the Greek language was spoken at least as far back as the thirteenth century BC, events of 350 BC–AD 300, notably the conquests of Alexander the Great (336–323 BC), shaped the development of New Testament Greek. Simply put, his diverse troops had to communicate with one another, and over time, the close contact contributed to the formation of a melting-pot Greek which came to be known as *Koiné* (Greek for "common"). Eventually, the inhabitants of conquered cities and colonies adopted *Koiné* Greek as a second language, often considered the civilized language. By the first century AD, it was the standard language of commerce in the Mediterranean region.

Both Greek speakers and Latin speakers shared similar social institutions. One such institution was the patron-client system or patronage. Patronage is a sort of collectivistic means of self-help in which a person in need has recourse to a higher-status person for some goods or services that are not available to the one in need or not available at the time. Since the patronage system was common in the Mediterranean culture area, it is no surprise that a set of cognate terms existed to express relations. For example, *prostatis* is the Greek translation of the Latin word *patrona*, the feminine form of *patronus*, meaning "patron," and *patronus* is a modification of the Latin word *pater*, meaning "father." The Greek cognate word for "father" is *patēr*. Notice the similarity in the Latin and Greek words for "father" and the connection between "patron" and "father." In the Roman Empire, the *paterfamilias* (head of the household) functioned as a patron to members of his extended family.[11]

The verb that corresponds to the noun *prostatis* is *proistēmi* and means "to exercise a position of leadership, to rule, direct, be at the head of,"[12] and forms of this verb occur in the New Testament. In his first letter to the Thessalonians, for example, Paul exhorts his readers to respect those who labor among them, those who are over them (*proistamenous*) in the Lord, and those who admonish them (1 Thess 5:12). Here we have three kinds of leaders who are able to informally influence the behavior and attitudes of others, usually because they are wealthy, act as patrons for those in their charge, or possess greater knowledge of Israel's traditions.[13] While Paul holds formal authority over Christ-believers in Thessalonica because he first proclaimed the forthcoming kingdom of God to them, these leaders, known as opinion leaders, exercise informal authority over the group, an authority fed by their interpersonal skills and connections with Paul. They emerge as leaders when Paul is away.

The verb *proistēmi* is also used in the New Testament to express the qualifications expected of overseers (1 Tim 3:4-5). Only the one who manages (*proistamenon*) the household well is fit for such a leadership role in the Jesus group. "Deacons"—or, more correctly, "go-betweens" or "agents"—must fulfill the same expectation; they must manage (*proistamenoi*) their children and households well (1 Tim 3:12). Furthermore, elders who rule (*proestōtes*) well by being exemplary teachers and preachers are said to be worthy of a double dose of honor (1 Tim 5:17). Overseers (*episkopoi*), elders (*presbuteroi*), and agents (*diakonoi*) represent three types of opinion leaders, individuals who possess the necessary qualifications to exercise informal authority within groups.

While Paul holds formal authority over the Jesus group in Kenchreai, Phoebe, as *diakonos*, is an opinion leader who exercises informal leadership in the assembly, particularly in Paul's absence. This is not to say that Phoebe—or any other opinion leader at this time—held an ecclesial office such as bishop, priest, or deacon as we know them today. While roles like *diakonos* seem to have acquired a more formal or institutionalized function by the end of the first century AD (1 Tim 3:11), they were more fluid in the middle of the first century. Nevertheless, as an opinion leader, Phoebe's status and authority in the assembly of Christ-believers at Kenchreai were substantial. Moreover, her function as emissary suggests that her influence was not limited to Kenchreai.

What then does Paul's descriptor *prostatis* add to our portrait of Phoebe? To begin with, a papyrus from 142 BC, which mentions a woman who was appointed the legal *prostatis* of her fatherless son, provides evidence that women could exercise legal functions such as guardianship.[14] As we have seen, both the noun *prostatis* and its related verb are used to describe individuals in positions of authority. The noun is used for Roman officials, benefactors, and patrons, while the verb expresses the kind of authority expected of opinion leaders in the Jesus group. As noted, those conversant with Israel's traditions and possessing plentiful resources were most likely to emerge as opinion leaders. There is reason to believe that Phoebe was a woman of means who belonged to the local elite of Kenchreai. Gerd Theissen, using four criteria (holding offices, owning houses, providing assistance to congregations, and freedom to travel) assesses the social position of the seventeen named Christ-believers in the Corinthian Jesus groups. Phoebe is numbered among the seventeen because she is associated with Kenchreai, which was closely associated with Corinth. On the basis of two of these criteria—service to Paul and the community, and freedom to travel—Theissen concludes that Phoebe is one of nine Corinthians hailing from the elite sector of society.[15] If he is correct, Phoebe very likely had the social connections and resources necessary to function not only as an opinion leader but also as a patron. Since in antiquity, patronage existed in more than one form, a brief sketch is necessary if we wish to speculate about the kind of patronage Phoebe exercised.

Patronage

By and large, in North American society, people dislike the practice of patronage. We are all familiar, for example, with job searches where better-qualified individuals are passed over in favor of others. Unless there are convincing reasons for such outcomes, our reaction is usually one of suspicion and lack of confidence in the hiring process. Hiring, we believe, ought to depend on applicants' qualifications. When it appears to be based on favoritism, the saying "It is not what you know but who you know" is often quoted. In Phoebe's world, however, patronage was an acceptable and very public means by which the majority of people acquired resources such as employment, promotions, debt relief, arable land, protection, or goods needed for the well-being of their families. Why was patronage the accepted and acceptable norm? Resources were limited and were controlled by a very small percentage of the population. In order to support themselves and their families, most people needed patrons who could assist them with gaining access to resources above and beyond the bare necessities. Those lacking a patron sought out those who could help them find one. These latter individuals exercised a form of patronage known as brokerage. Brokers (in Latin: *mediator*) had access to resources and to powerful patrons with even more resources; brokers served, therefore, as go-betweens or agents on behalf of others.

When a patron granted a favor, the individual receiving the favor became a client of the patron, and the relationship that developed was defined by certain characteristics.[16] First, although patron and client could have the same, or close to the same, social status, the patron's social status was often higher. Hence, even though the word "friendship" was used of their relationship, patron and client were not friends as we understand that term today. We typically think of our friends as social equals. In Phoebe's time, while people had friends who were their social equals, patrons and their clients were political friends, and clients sought to honor their patrons for favors received. But the patron-client relationship was also a personal one; the patron functioned like a powerful family member who controlled access to resources and treated clients like dependants. Moreover, the relationship was often long-term, in fact, so long-term that clients were sometimes passed on from one generation of patrons to the next.[17] Finally, the relationship was reciprocal; while good patrons helped their clients gain needed resources, good clients, as we shall see, returned the favor by whatever means possible, especially by public expressions of praise and support.

Ideally, patronage was motivated by true generosity. In fact, there is a direct connection between patronage and the favors that patrons grant. The Latin word for "favor" is *gratia*, in Greek, *charis*. It thus refers to patronage. A favor (or grace) is something that one cannot attain unless another gives it. A patron is one who is in the position to give and by doing so demonstrates favoritism toward the client. Hence, the act of patronage and the gifts that flow from it constitute favoritism or grace (*charis*).[18]

Biblical authors stress the importance of generosity, teaching that the truly generous individual does not give for selfish reasons: "A fool's gift will profit you nothing, for he has many eyes instead of one. He gives little and upbraids much, he opens his mouth like a herald; today he lends and tomorrow he asks it back; such a one is a hateful man" (Sir 20:14-15). According to Ben Sira, such an individual draws attention to the act of giving and hopes to profit by it, thereby acting shamefully. The honorable patron, however, avoids the temptation to be self-seeking and gives graciously. This does not mean that patrons handed out economic and political resources and received nothing in return: social expectations were placed on the client who received a gift. An honorable client expressed gratitude and reciprocated by whatever means possible, thereby practicing the virtue of justice.[19] Clients typically demonstrated their gratitude by publicly praising patrons for their largesse. Even a very poor client could afford such an expression of solidarity and loyalty, and this served to increase the patron's honor in the eyes of others. Ungrateful clients were considered shameful individuals, and since no one wanted to be labeled in this way and shunned by others, the pressure to respond appropriately to gifts was substantial.

The patron-client relationship, therefore, was a reciprocal relationship. Basically, the client was to return a favor in equal measure; this is known as balanced reciprocity.[20] Compare this with what Luke's Jesus has to say about giving: "If you do good to those who do good to you, what credit is that to you? For even sinners do the same. And if you lend to those from whom you hope to receive, what credit is that to you? Even sinners lend to sinners, to receive as much again. But love your enemies, and do good, and lend, expecting nothing in return; and your reward will be great, and you will be sons of the Most High; for he is kind to the ungrateful and the selfish. Be merciful, even as your Father is merciful" (Luke 6:33-36). The kind of reciprocity that Luke describes here is known as generalized reciprocity; one gives without expectation of return. This was the way that family members and friends (social equals) interacted. We learned earlier that Jesus groups functioned like families; they were fictive families, and their members were to treat one another as if they were members of the same biological family. Hence, Luke reminds those who are well-off that they are to give to their brothers and sisters in faith without looking for anything in return.

Patronage is also an important aspect of worship. The belief that blessings and gifts are God-given puts the gods in the role of patron and humanity in the role of client. The proper response to the patronage of the gods was one of gratitude expressed as worship. According to the gospels, Jesus instructed his disciples to address God as their *patēr* (Matt 6:9). This word, meaning "father" or "patron," is a way of addressing God that recognizes God's gifts or patronage.[21] In essence, members of Jesus groups envisioned God as the ultimate patron and Jesus as the broker through whom humanity gained access to God's grace or favors. Jesus' role as broker is spelled out by the Fourth Evangelist: "For the law was given through Moses; grace and truth came through Jesus Christ" (John 1:17). The grace to which the evangelist refers is God's patronage with Jesus as broker. Consider 1 Timothy also: "For there is one God, and there is one mediator between God and men, the man Christ Jesus" (1 Tim 2:5-6).

Benefaction

Another kind of reciprocity typical of elites in the Greco-Roman world is benefaction. A benefactor (*euergetēs* in the cognate Greek) was a wealthy patron who supported associations, towns, or cities by performing some sort of exceptional service on their behalf, such as the erection of public buildings, payment for public festivals, or the public distribution of food.[22] In return, they received honors, such as inscriptions that praised their generosity, public proclamations, crowns, or seats of honor in the theater during civic festivities. Benefaction was driven by the desire for honor. In fact, the word *philotimia* ("love of honor") was one of the names for public benefaction.[23] But while the relationship between benefactor and the local public could endure over time, it was not a personal relationship. Consider, for example, the centurion who facilitates the building of the synagogue for the Israelites of Capernaum (Luke 7:5); he is a benefactor, yet his story is told as that of a patron.

This centurion's highly regarded slave is dying. Hearing of Jesus' reputation as a folk healer, the centurion sends the village elders to him. Their role is to act as intermediaries who will broker a favor from Jesus. By acting as brokers on his behalf, the elders acknowledge the centurion's patronage (benefaction) to Capernaum. Their mission is successful. Jesus agrees to accompany them to the centurion's home. Before they reach the house, however, friends (in this case social equals) of the centurion relay a message: "I am not worthy to have you come under my roof" (Luke 7:6). By these words, the centurion signals that he has no intention of making Jesus a client.[24] Instead, he regards Jesus as his superior, his patron. Amazed by the man's trust in his ability to broker God's healing power, Jesus heals the slave. In this story, the centurion is a benefactor-patron whose generosity motivates the elders to attempt to broker a favor for him from Jesus, the holy man with access to God's power of healing. Both Jesus and the elders exercise brokerage by acting as go-betweens: the elders broker a favor from Jesus for the centurion, and Jesus brokers a favor from God for the centurion. Similarly, acting as emissary for the Jesus group in Kenchreai, Phoebe brokers the assistance of Ephesian Jesus groups. To promote her success, Paul acts as her broker by writing a letter of recommendation in which he praises her as *diakonos* and *prostatis* and exhorts the Ephesians to help her "in whatever matter she may have need of you."

While the purpose of Phoebe's visit is not stated, Paul's use of the word *pragma* has sparked some reflection. Generally speaking, *pragma* means "thing, matter, task, affair" but carries the more specific meaning of "dispute, lawsuit." If the latter meaning is intended, Phoebe is probably acting as a litigant.[25]

Women and Patronage

The public activities of first-century Mediterranean men and women were largely determined by the honor ratings of their families. The way people dressed, their gestures, their right to speak, when they spoke, the people with whom they transacted business deals, those with whom they ate, and where they reclined at meals constitute just a few of the social activities predetermined by their honor rating.[26] One's life, then, was hugely influenced by one's social status.

Generally speaking, women belonged to one of four social categories: aristocratic, freedwomen, free women, or slaves.[27] Aristocratic women comprised a very small percentage of the population in the Roman Empire. By the first century BC, they had the right to initiate divorce, to own property, and to inherit land and money. Freedwomen were women born into slavery who eventually garnered the necessary resources to buy their freedom. While they had less status than aristocratic women, some gained considerable wealth as merchants of upscale products while others continued to live and work in the households of their previous masters. Free women were born into families that varied greatly in wealth and social status. Like freedwomen, many worked in business and trade, sometimes with their husbands. Female slaves carried out many tasks within the household. Since slaves were owned by others and believed to be devoid of honor, sexual availability of female slaves was taken for granted. They lacked the right to protect their chastity,[28] a virtue that helped to safeguard the legitimacy of their off-spring.

For the main part, a public-private division of labor influenced the place of women in first-century Mediterranean societies. In cities and towns, women were primarily associated with the household sphere and men with the city. Hence, while men moved freely about in open places such as the marketplace, respectable women were expected to manage the affairs of their households.[29] Women could not vote and were not elected to hold office. This does not mean, however, that women had no influence in public life. While the household was exclusively a private domain, it had political importance and influenced public discourses.[30] Moreover, women appeared before courts and were members of social organizations. They served as advisors to their husbands and sons and participated in public political discussions with them. While there is no evidence that women participated directly in city councils, and while most political offices in the Roman Empire were held by men, inscriptions from Asia Minor reveal that a small number of wealthy women were appointed by city councils to offices such as *hipparch* (highest civic office), *prytanis* (ruler), *stephanēphoros* (wreath bearer), *dekaprōtos* (member of finance committee), *demiurge* (artificer), *archon* (civic magistrate), *agonothete* (sponsor of contests), *panēguriarchēs* (sponsor of sacrifices and banquets), *gymnasiarch* (ruler of cultural and educational center), *timouchos* (honor holder), *archiereia* (priestess), *strategos* (member of magisterial board), *gerousiarchissa* (president of the council of elders), *Lyciarch* (presiding officer over Federation of Lycia), *Pontarch* (presiding officer over Federation of Pontus), and *Asiarch* (highest provincial office in Asia Minor).[31] Honorary appointments such as these were bestowed on women (and men) in return for their civic benefactions. Gratitude was also frequently expressed by the erection of statues of benefactors and public inscriptions expounding their generosity. The following inscription, which testifies to the benefaction of Claudia Metrodora, serves to illustrate the kinds of offices bestowed on elite women in return for their benefactions:

For Claudia Metrodora, daughter of Skytheinos, gymnasiarch four times [who] twice distributed oil to the city on the occasion of the festival of the heraklea games; agonothete three times of the Heraklea Romaia and Kaisareia; queen of the thirteen cities of the Ionian federation, being desirous of glory for the city, . . . a lover of her homeland and priestess for life of the divine empress Aphrodite Livia, by reason of her excellence and admirable behavior towards it.[32]

As we try to understand how women were involved in the sphere traditionally reserved for men, it is important to know that the social freedom of women varied throughout the Greco-Roman empire. About four centuries before Phoebe's lifetime, Hellenistic ("Greek") philosophers viewed women as property to be transferred from father to husband at marriage.[33] While Plato and Aristotle made efforts to define the place of women in society, they still maintained the superiority of men over women and the political power of men over their wives within the household. Women, by their nature, were deemed inferior to men. By the second century BC, the first attempts to define the mutual relations of husband and wife were made and the place of affection in the conjugal relationship was recognized. Nevertheless, the man was still the point of reference.

By the first century AD, Roman women were able to exercise a measure of financial independence and enjoyed more social freedom than in previous centuries.[34] The patronage they could exercise took on a variety of forms. According to Bruce W. Winter, "it was not inappropriate for a wife to present petitions to her husband about matters of public policy, to intercede with him on behalf of individuals, to lend money to people outside her own family, to make generous gifts of cash both to cities and individuals, to undertake building projects in her own name and at her own expense, and still to be presented in public as the embodiment of a wife's traditional virtues."[35] Women, it seems, were able to act as patrons of individuals and to engage in civic benefactions. Their influence in public matters was strongest in areas such as Corinth, Philippi, and the Roman province of Asia where Roman influence heavily outweighed any other.[36] During the first century, the women of Kenchreai, one of the major Roman ports in the Corinthia, likely enjoyed a relatively high degree of social freedom, particularly if they, like Phoebe, were women of means.

Phoebe as Patron

Paul's designation of Phoebe as *prostatis* honors her as a patron. By referring to her in this manner, he acknowledges that he and many others are somehow socially dependent on her. Interestingly, one of Phoebe's contemporaries, the wealthy Iunia Theodora who lived in nearby Corinth, is described by the word *prostasian* ("patronage"), a cognate of *prostatis* ("patron"). It is thought that Iunia was not only a Roman citizen, but a citizen of Corinth who was originally from a city in Lycia;[37] her Lycian origins would explain her loyalty to Lycian travelers passing through Corinth. Five different inscriptions found on a single *stele* (a commemorative stone with an inscribed surface that is set into the facade of a building) testify to her agency on behalf of Lycian merchants and travelers. One reads as follows:[38]

> In the fourth year, when Dionysophanes, son of . . . was priest, the council and people of Telmessos decreed, the proposal of the pyrtaneis . . . : Since Iunia Theodora, a Roman, a benefactress of the greatest loyalty to the Lycian federation and our city has accomplished numerous . . . benefits for the federation and our city and, dwelling in the city of the Corinthians welcomes in her own house Lycian travelers and our citizens . . . supplying them with everything . . . ; displaying her patronage [*prostasian*] of those who are present . . . of her own love of fame and assiduousness . . . , it is decreed that our city in its turn testify to her according to her deserts; by good fortune, it pleases

> the demos of Telmessos to give honor and praise for all the
> above reasons to the above-mentioned Iunia Theodora and
> to invite her, living with the same intentions, to always be
> the author of some benefit toward us, well knowing that
> in return our city recognizes and will acknowledge the
> evidence of her goodwill.[39]

Telmessos was an important city in Lycia. According to the inscription cited above, Iunia's patronage included hospitality to
Lycian travelers and the provision of whatever they needed. On
a number of occasions, she represented the commercial interests
of Lycia by gaining the favor of Roman officials toward Lycian
sailors and their cargo. Corinth and its major ports controlled
the movement of goods between Italy and the Aegean Sea, particularly because of the Diolkos (mentioned previously) that
allowed ships to circumvent the dangerous trip around the
southern tip of the Peloponnesus. An agent who could guarantee
one a safer route was a tremendous asset.

As with Phoebe, there is no indication that Iunia's patronage
was connected in any way to the activities of a husband or son.
One of the inscriptions (a letter from the Lycian city of Myra to
Corinth) mentions Iunia's father Lucius, but the praise expressed
in the inscription is directed solely at Iunia for her support of
Lycian citizens in Corinth. Another inscription (a letter from the
Federal Assembly to Corinth introducing a second decree in
favor of Iunia Theodora) mentions a man, Sextus Iulius, who is
her heir but presumably not her son. By the first century AD,
both the independence and public visibility of wives and widows were on the increase in the Roman Empire.[40] Considering
that no mention is made of husbands and that Iunia and Phoebe
are described as if they are agents in their own right, these
women were probably widows.

Paul's recommendation (Rom 16:1-2) implies that Phoebe
serves as a personal patron of many people, including Paul himself. While we cannot rule out the possibility that Phoebe and
other Christ-believers engaged in civic benefaction in ways

comparable to that of Iunia Theodora, there is as yet no inscriptional evidence that expressly identifies civic benefactors as members of Jesus groups. In fact, civic patronage may not have been an option open to Christianity until later centuries. Instead, early Christ-believers of means likely extended patronage to other Jesus-group members by offering hospitality, hosting group meetings, and providing "material and cash gifts, food and dinner invitations, lodging, favorable recommendations and appointments, help in matchmaking, and bequests and inheritances."[41] Often their resources went to less fortunate individuals and Jesus groups.[42] In all likelihood, Phoebe's patronage benefited both individuals and the Jesus group at Kenchreai.

While Phoebe probably provided financial support for some people, it is doubtful that she did so for Paul, because in the Corinthian correspondence, Paul emphasizes that he has not received any financial assistance from Corinthian Jesus groups (2 Cor 11:9); the Jesus groups of Macedonia (north of Achaia) paid Paul for his services. It is plausible to imagine, however, that Phoebe was one of the first in Kenchreai to accept Paul's proclamation of the kingdom and enabled him to make the social connections necessary to establish the first Jesus group in the city. As a woman of means, Phoebe would have owned a house large enough to host meetings and to provide lodging for Paul and other itinerant Christ-believers. As *diakonos* she (and perhaps others) could oversee the assembly in his absence and keep him informed of their progress. She also traveled on behalf of the Jesus group in Kenchreai and represented their interests to other groups. In return, Paul sang the praises of his patron to his Ephesian coworkers—she was "sister," *diakonos*, and *prostatis*.

CONCLUSION

As I was writing this book, people often inquired about its subject. Almost without fail, my reply sparked wonderment that someone would choose to write a book about a character about whom so little textual evidence exists. It has been, I admit, a challenge, but one that has been greatly ameliorated with the help of social-scientific criticism and the published findings of archaeological digs at ancient Kenchreai.

Biblical texts, such as Paul's letter to the Romans, are known as high-context documents. As such, the writers do not provide information that is common knowledge to them and their addressees. While it is tempting for us to fill in the gaps by recourse to our own social system, we must resist the temptation, realizing that we are foreigners in the land of the Bible. Unlike our low-context world of today, which is inundated by the written word, Phoebe's high-context world was primarily oral. Information was received and passed on predominantly by word of mouth. While our obsession with written information may tempt us to judge this as inefficient, New Testament writers were not under that impression. Numerous examples of the effectiveness of oral communication can be found in the epistles and gospels. One case occurs in Paul's expression of gratitude for his Roman addressees because "your faith is proclaimed in all the world" (Rom 1:8). In other words, reports of their faith are spreading throughout the Roman Empire by word of mouth. As another example, the evangelists frequently say that news of Jesus' effectiveness as a folk healer spreads rapidly. In fact, despite Jesus' insistence that people remain silent about his won-drous deeds, they go away and spread the news anyway. The healing of the leper provides a good example: "And immediately the leprosy left him, and he was made clean. And he [Jesus] sternly charged him, and sent him away at once, and said to him, 'See that you say nothing to anyone; but go, show yourself to the priest, and offer for your cleansing what Moses com-manded, for a proof to the people.' But he went out and began to talk freely about it, and to spread the news, so that Jesus could no longer openly enter a town, but was out in the country; and people came to him from every quarter" (Mark 1:42-45).

The effectiveness of oral communication helps us to speculate reasonably about how Phoebe and Paul came to be coworkers in the spread of the gospel. In approximately AD 50, Paul first arrived in Corinth. According to Luke, Paul proclaimed and explained the gospel there for eighteen months (Acts 18:11). During that time, he faced some opposition (18:5-6) but had much success as well. In the synagogue, many Israelite Judeans and Hellenists were persuaded by his preaching (18:4). He also preached next door in the house of Titius Justus (18:7) where Crispus, the ruler of the synagogue, accepted the gospel; he and his entire household were baptized (18:8). Many other Corin-thians, upon hearing Paul, believed and were baptized (18:8). With so many people hearing and embracing the gospel in Corinth, word of Paul's preaching would have soon reached Kenchreai, only nine kilometers away.

With Luke's account in mind, we offer two speculative recon-structions of how Paul met Phoebe. First, literary and archaeo-logical evidence indicates that Kenchreai was an important Corinthian port that served the Peloponnesus and centers to the east, something that would have made it an attractive location for Paul to proclaim the gospel. Its proximity to Corinth supports the proposition that while Paul was in Corinth, he also pro-claimed and taught the gospel of the God of Israel in Kenchreai. There he met Phoebe along with other Israelites who became disciples of Christ. During the many months that Paul spent in the Corinthia, he probably visited Kenchreai more than once, perhaps lodging in Phoebe's house when in town. As one of the few elite Corinthian Christ-believers, Phoebe soon became a *diakonos* in the assembly at Kenchreai, serving as opinion leader, patron, and emissary when necessary.

Barring the possibility that Paul visited Kenchreai before he left Corinth, we offer a second hypothetical scenario. After a successful preaching mission, Paul, Prisca, and Aquila left Corinth for Ephesus (Acts 18:19). On the way, they stopped at Kenchreai (18:18) where Paul cut his hair because of a vow, perhaps a Nazirite vow by which he had dedicated himself to God for a specified period of time (Num 6:1-21). By the time they arrived in Kenchreai en route to Ephesus, Paul's reputation and success preceded him. Before leaving Kenchreai, he proclaimed the gospel among Israelites there. Phoebe, an elite woman of means, became a Christ-believer. She acted as Paul's patron by providing him lodging while he was in town. In his absence, she emerged as an opinion leader within the congregation.

The plausibility of these scenarios is supported by Luke's account of Lydia, a seller of purple goods living in Philippi. Lydia and a number of other Israelite women heard Paul's proclamation of the gospel of the God of Israel. Subsequently, she and her household were baptized, and Lydia invited Paul and his companions to stay in her home (Acts 16:14-15).

Phoebe, an elite woman introduced by Paul as "sister," *diakonos*, and *prostatis*, was a coworker of Paul and an informal leader in the Jesus group at Kenchreai. Hailing from the local elites, Phoebe was probably literate and well connected socially, therefore eminently qualified to serve as patron and as emissary on behalf of her community, even if that representation involved litigation. She was probably not a young, unmarried woman. For both Mediterranean men and women, honor increases with age, and for women, it also increases with the birth of each son. Like her contemporary, Iunia Theodora, Phoebe appears to have been unattached to a husband. Since the vast majority of women married, Phoebe was most likely an influential, elite widow who used her resources to benefit members of Jesus groups. A leading force in the spread of the gospel throughout the Corinthia, Phoebe of Kenchreai was a loyal and valued associate of Paul. Her story, coming to light again after two thousand years, will endure long after the legacy of the glamorous Phoebe Snow has been forgotten.

> Kenchreai, town
> Of great renown
> Saronic port
> And Phoebe's crown,
> 'Tis there she's called
> Sister of all
> *Diakonos*,
> Patron of Paul.
>
> As go-between
> And broker queen,
> This Radiant One
> Is often seen;
> Like Phoebe Snow
> She's on the go,
> But Ephesus,
> Not Buffalo.

NOTES

Introduction, pages 1–18

1. Margaret Young, "On the Go with Phoebe Snow: Origins of an Advertising Icon," *Advertising and Society Review* 7 (2006): 12, 23.

2. Ibid., 1.

3. Some sources employ the spelling "Cenchreae" and others "Kenchreai." In this book, we use "Kenchreai," except in quotations where the other spelling is used.

4. Bruce J. Malina, "The Social Sciences and Biblical Interpretation," *Interpretation* 36 (1982): 229–42.

5. Raphael Patai, *The Arab Mind*, rev. ed. (New York: Hatherleigh Press, 2002), 180–87.

6. David Rhoads, "Performance Criticism: An Emerging Methodology in Second Testament Studies—Part I," *Biblical Theology Bulletin* 36 (2006): 118.

7. Ibid., 121.

8. K. C. Hanson and Douglas E. Oakman, *Palestine in the Time of Jesus: Social Structures and Social Conflicts* (Minneapolis, MN: Fortress Press, 1998), 194.

9. Bedouin are inhabitants of the desert, particularly the desert-dwelling nomads of Arabia, the Negev, and the Sinai.

10. Bruce J. Malina and Richard L. Rohrbaugh, *Social-Science Commentary on the Synoptic Gospels*, 2nd ed. (Minneapolis, MN: Fortress Press, 2003), 3–5.

11. Raphael Patai, *Family, Love, and the Bible* (London: Macgibbon and Kee, 1960), 13.

12. Papyrus Oxyrhynchus 744.G.

13. Amal Rassam, "Women and Domestic Power in Morocco," *International Journal of Middle Eastern Studies* 12 (1980): 176.

14. There is scholarly consensus that Paul wrote 1 Thessalonians, 1 and 2 Corinthians, Galatians, Romans, Philippians, and Philemon. Opinion is divided regarding other New Testament letters that are often attributed to him.

15. Robert Jewett, "Paul, Phoebe, and the Spanish Mission," in *The Social World of Formative Christianity and Judaism: Essays in Tribute to Howard Clark Kee*, ed. Jacob Neusner (Philadelphia, PA: Fortress Press, 1988), 144.

16. Philip F. Esler, *Conflict and Identity in Romans: The Social Setting of Paul's Letter* (Minneapolis, MN: Fortress Press, 2003), 12.

17. Bruce J. Malina and John J. Pilch, *Social-Science Commentary on the Letters of Paul* (Minneapolis, MN: Fortress Press, 2006), 3–4.

18. Ibid.

19. Esler, *Conflict*, 358–59.

20. See, for example, James D. G. Dunn, *Romans 9–16*, Word Biblical Commentary 38B (Dallas, TX: Word Books, 1988), 886; Joseph A. Fitzmyer, *Romans: A New Translation with Introduction and Commentary*, Anchor Bible 33 (New York: Doubleday, 1993), 729.

21. Jewett, "Spanish Mission," 151.

22. Fitzmyer, *Romans*, 85.

23. Ancient Corinth was destroyed by earthquakes in AD 375 and 551. Centuries later (AD 1858), the old city was completely destroyed by an earthquake. The new city of Corinth was founded on the coast of the Gulf of Corinth, less than two miles southwest of the site of ancient Corinth.

24. Fitzmyer, *Romans*, 49.

25. Romans 16:24 is not included in Greek manuscripts that retain the doxology at 16:25-27, probably because it introduces redundancy. You will find that many English translations of Romans also omit 16:24, most likely for the same reason.

26. For a thorough attempt to delineate the text of Romans and the reasons for and against the inclusion of chapter 16, see Fitzmyer, *Romans*, 44-67.

27. Malina and Pilch, *Letters of Paul*, 291–92.

28. Jerome Murphy-O'Connor, *St. Paul's Ephesus: Texts and Archaeology* (Collegeville, MN: Liturgical Press, 2008), 16.

29. In the letter to the Romans, Paul identifies her as Prisca (Rom 16:3) but, here in Acts, Luke uses the diminutive form, "Priscilla" (Acts 18:2) or "Little Prisca."

30. Bruce J. Malina, *Timothy: Paul's Closest Associate*, Paul's Social Network: Brothers and Sisters in Faith (Collegeville, MN: Liturgical Press, 2008), x.

31. Johannes P. Louw and Eugene A. Nida, eds., *Greek-English Lexicon of the New Testament: Based on Semantic Domains*, 2nd ed. (New York: United Bible Societies, 1989), 125.

Chapter 1, pages 19–32

1. Chan-Hie Kim, *Form and Structure of the Familiar Greek Letter of Recommendation*, SBLDS 4 (Missoula, MT: SBL, 1972).

2. For a more in-depth discussion of individualism and collectivism, see Bruce J. Malina, *Timothy: Paul's Closest Associate*, Paul's Social Network: Brothers and Sisters in Faith (Collegeville, MN: Liturgical Press, 2008), 1–20; and John J. Pilch, *Stephen: Paul and the Hellenist Israelites*, Paul's Social Network: Brothers and Sisters in Faith (Collegeville, MN: Liturgical Press, 2008), 17–35.

3. David G. Horrell, "From ἀδελφοί to οἶκος θεοῦ: Social Transformation in Pauline Christianity," *Journal of Biblical Literature* 120, no. 2 (2001): 296.

4. Raphael Patai, *Golden River to Golden Road: Society, Culture, and Change in the Middle East*, 3rd ed. (Philadelphia: University of Pennsylvania Press, 1969), 84–94.

5. Julian Pitt-Rivers, "Honour and Social Status," in *Honour and Shame: The Values of Mediterranean Society*, ed. J. G. Péristiany (Chicago, IL: University of Chicago Press, 1966), 21.

6. Bruce J. Malina, *The New Testament World: Insights from Cultural Anthropology*, 3rd ed. (Louisville, KY: Westminster John Knox Press, 2001), 32–33.

7. Julian Pitt-Rivers, *The Fate of Shechem or the Politics of Sex: Essays in the Anthropology of the Mediterranean*, Cambridge Studies in Social and Cultural Anthropology Series 19, ed. Jack Goody (Cambridge: Cambridge University Press, 1977), xi, 1.

8. John H. Elliott, *What is Social-Scientific Criticism?* (Minneapolis, MN: Fortress Press, 1993), 130.

9. Juliet Du Boulay, *Portrait of a Greek Mountain Village* (Oxford: Clarendon Press, 1974), 21–22, 142–43.

10. Bruce J. Malina and Richard L. Rohrbaugh, *Social-Science Commentary on the Synoptic Gospels*, 2nd ed. (Minneapolis, MN: Fortress Press, 2003), 288–90.

11. Valeria Finucci, *The Manly Masquerade: Masculinity, Paternity, and Castration in the Italian Renaissance* (Durham, NC: Duke University Press, 2003), 9–11.

12. Fred Eggan, "Kinship: Introduction," in *International Encyclopedia of the Social Sciences*, ed. David L. Sills (New York: Macmillan and the Free Press, 1968), 8:390–92.

13. Dennis C. Duling, "The Matthean Brotherhood and Marginal Scribal Leadership," in *Modelling Early Christianity: Social-Scientific Studies of the New Testament in Its Context*, ed. Philip F. Esler (New York: Routledge, 1995), 159–82.

14. Julian Pitt-Rivers, "Kinship: Pseudo-Kinship," in *International Encyclopedia of the Social Sciences*, 8:408–13.

15. Plutarch, The Education of Children, 7.D-E, cited from Frank Cole Babbitt, trans., *Moralia*, vol. 1 (London: William Heinemann, 1927), 35.

16. Dennis C. Duling, "Recruitment in the Jesus Movement in Social-Scientific Perspective," in *Social Scientific Models for Interpreting the Bible: Essays by the Context Group in Honor of Bruce J. Malina*, ed. John J. Pilch (Leiden: E. J. Brill, 2001), 157.

17. Bruce J. Malina, "Love," in Bruce J. Malina and John J. Pilch, eds., *Handbook of Biblical Social Values*, rev. ed. (Peabody, MA: Hendrickson, 1998), 129.

18. Malina and Rohrbaugh, *Synoptic Gospels*, 156.

19. Frederick William Danker, ed., *A Greek-English Lexicon of the New Testament and Other Early Christian Literature* (BDAG), 3rd ed. (Chicago, IL: University of Chicago Press, 2000), 18.

20. S. Scott Bartchy, "Undermining Ancient Patriarchy: The Apostle Paul's Vision of a Society of Siblings," *Biblical Theology Bulletin* 29 (1999): 68.

21. Ibid., 71.

22. Duling, "Recruitment," 158.

23. Ibid., 69.

Chapter 2, pages 33–46

1. Richard L. Rohrbaugh, "Introduction," in *The Social Sciences and New Testament Interpretation*, ed. Richard L. Rohrbaugh (Peabody, MA: Hendrickson, 1996), 7.

2. Mary Ann Foley, "Culture Area," in *Encyclopedia of Anthropology*, ed. David E. Hunter and Phillip Whitten (New York: Harper and Row, 1976), 104.

3. Stanley Brandes, "Reflections on Honor and Shame in the Mediterranean," in *Honor and Shame and the Unity of the Mediterranean*, ed. David D. Gilmore (Washington, DC: American Anthropological Association, 1987), 121–22.

4. James Wiseman, *The Land of the Ancient Corinthians*, Studies in Mediterranean Archeology 50 (Göteborg: Paul Åström, 1978), 10.

5. J. B. Salmon, *Wealthy Corinth: A History of the City to 338 BC* (Oxford: Clarendon Press, 1984), 1, 8.

6. Jerome Murphy-O'Connor, *St. Paul's Corinth: Texts and Archaeology* (Collegeville, MN: Liturgical Press, 2002), 58.

7. Charles H. Miller, "Corinth," in *Harper's Bible Commentary*, ed. Paul J. Achtemeier (San Francisco: Harper and Row, 1985), 182.

8. Clyde E. Fant and Mitchell G. Reddish, *A Guide to Biblical Sites in Greece and Turkey* (New York: Oxford University Press, 2003), 46.

9. Robert L. Hohlfelder, "Kenchreai on the Saronic Gulf: Aspects of its Imperial History," *The Classical Journal* 71 (1976): 218.

10. Wilma Olch Stern and Danae Hadjilazaro Thimme, *Ivory, Bone, and Related Wood Finds*, vol. 6, *Kenchreai: Eastern Port of Corinth* (Leiden: E. J. Brill, 2007), 1.

11. Thucydides, *History of the Peloponnesian War: Books III and IV*, trans. Charles Forster Smith (Cambridge, MA: Harvard University Press, 1975), 289.

12. Hohlfelder, "Kenchreai on the Saronic Gulf," 220.

13. Salmon, *Wealthy Corinth*, 31.

14. Fant and Reddish, *Biblical Sites*, 42.

15. Robert L. Hohlfelder, *The Coins*, vol. 3, *Kenchreai: Eastern Port of Corinth* (Leiden: E. J. Brill, 1978), 2.

16. Richard M. Rothaus, *Corinth: The First City of Greece: An Urban History of Late Antique Cult and Religion* (Leiden: E. J. Brill, 2000), 29, 66.

17. Robert Scranton, Joseph W. Shaw, and Leila Ibrahim, *Topography and Architecture*, vol. 1, *Kenchreai: Eastern Port of Corinth* (Leiden: E. J. Brill, 1978), 6.

18. Murphy-O'Connor, *Paul's Corinth*, 19.

19. Hohlfelder, "Kenchreai on the Saronic Gulf," 222.

20. Murphy-O'Connor, *Paul's Corinth*, 52–53.

21. Cited from Horace Leonard Jones, trans., *The Geography of Strabo*, vol. 4 (Cambridge, MA: Harvard University Press, 1988), 189, 195, 197.

22. Henry George Liddell and Robert Scott, *Greek-English Lexicon with a Revised Supplement* (Oxford: Clarendon Press, 1996), 1216.

23. Wiseman, *Ancient Corinthians*, 45.

24. Walter Werner, "The Largest Ship Trackway in Ancient Times: The Diolkos of the Isthmus of Corinth, Greece, and Early Attempts to Build a Canal," *The International Journal of Nautical Archaeology* 26 (1977): 106.

25. Ibid., 114.

26. Apuleius of Madauros, *The Transformation of Lucius Otherwise Known as The Golden Ass*, trans. Robert Graves (New York: Farrar, Straus, and Giroux, 1951), 255–81.

27. Apuleius of Madauros, *The Isis Book: Metamorphoses, Book XI*, ed. and trans. J. Gwyn Griffiths (Leiden: E. J. Brill, 1975), 75, 77.

28. Ibid., 15.

29. Cited from W. H. S. Jones, trans., *Pausanias: Description of Greece*, vol. 1 (Cambridge, MA: Harvard University Press, 1978), 255.

30. Scranton, *Kenchreai*, 79–98.

31. Rothaus, *Corinth*, 68.

32. Scranton, *Kenchreai*, 72.

33. Ibid., 73.

34. Rothaus, *Corinth*, 69–70.

35. John G. Hawthorne, "Cenchreae: Port of Corinth," *Archaeology* 18 (1965): 193.

36. Rothaus, *Corinth*, 77.

37. During the first century, groups were identified by the region of their origin. Even though many members of the house of Israel were scattered around the Mediterranean region, they were known as "Judeans" because, regardless of where they lived, they were still associated with the region of Judea, especially with Jerusalem and its magnificent temple. For more detail on this topic see Philip F. Esler, *Conflict and Identity in Romans: The Social Setting of Paul's Letter* (Minneapolis, MN: Fortress Press, 2003), 62–74.

38. Ibid., 90–107.

39. Cited from Robert Charles Hill, trans., *Theodoret of Cyrus: Commentary on the Letters of Saint Paul*, vol. 1 (Brookline, MA: Holy Cross Orthodox Press, 2001), 135.

40. Wiseman, *Ancient Corinthians*, 10.

Chapter 3, pages 47–77

1. Jeannine E. Olson, *Deacons and Deaconesses through the Centuries*, rev. ed. (Saint Louis, MO: Concordia Publishing House, 2005).

2. Ibid., 61.

3. For a more comprehensive discussion of the contents and significance of these documents, see Kyriaki Karidoyanes FitzGerald, *Women Deacons in the Orthodox Church: Called to Holiness and Ministry* (Brookline, MA: Holy Cross Orthodox Press, 1998), 18–27, 59–77.

4. R. Hugh Connolly, *Didascalia Apostolorum: The Syriac Version Translated and Accompanied by the Verona Latin Fragments* (Oxford: Clarendon Press, 1969), 147.

5. Kyriaki Karidoyanes FitzGerald, "Orthodox Women and Pastoral Practice: Observations and Concerns for the Church in America," *Saint Nina Quarterly* 3, no. 2 (1999). Online: http://www.stnina.org/journal/art/3.2.2.

6. Karidoyanes FitzGerald, *Women Deacons*, 21, 23, 49–50.

7. Ibid., 23.

8. Cited from Olson, *Deacons and Deaconesses*, 57.

9. Cited from Karidoyanes FitzGerald, *Women Deacons*, 203–4.

10. Becky Dodson Louter, "Office of Deaconess and Home Missioner Program," *Global Ministries: The United Methodist Church*. Online: http://new.gbgm-umc.org/about/us/mp/deaconess-homemissioner/.

11. James Monroe Barnett, *The Diaconate: A Full and Equal Order*, rev. ed. (Valley Forge, PA: Trinity Press International, 1995), 157.

12. Lutheran Deaconess Association, "What is a Lutheran Deaconess?" Online: http://www.thelda.org/about/what_is.php.

13. North American Association for the Diaconate, "Deacons in Anglican Churches." Online: http://www.diakonoi.org/naadinfo.html.

14. "The Permanent Diaconate Today: A Research Report by the Bishops' Committee on the Diaconate of the NCCB and by the Center for Applied Research in the Apostolate." Online: http://cara.georgetown.edu/pdfs/PermanentDiaconate.PDF.

15. Although two-thirds of the Presbyterians in Canada did enter this union, the other one-third became The Presbyterian Church in Canada, a denomination which still exists today.

16. Committee on Diaconal Ministry, *History of Diaconal Ministry in the United Church of Canada* (Saturna Island, BC: Division of Ministry Personnel and Education; The United Church of Canada, 1991), 1.

17. The United Church of Canada, "Discernment of Ministry: Diaconal Ministry." Online: http://www.united-church.ca/adultlearning/preparing/discernment/diaconal.

18. Cited from Origen, *Commentary on the Epistle to the Romans: Books 6–10*, trans. Thomas Scheck, The Fathers of the Church: A New Translation, vol. 104 (Washington, DC: Catholic University of America Press, 2002), 290–91.

19. Bruce J. Malina, "Hospitality," in *Handbook of Biblical Social Values*, eds. John J. Pilch and Bruce J. Malina (Peabody, MA: Hendrickson, 1998), 115–18.

20. Cited from Philip Schaff, ed., *A Select Library of the Post-Nicene Fathers of the Christian Church*, vol. 11 (New York: Christian Literature Company, 1889), 549–50.

21. John N. Collins, *Diakonia: Re-interpreting the Ancient Sources* (New York: Oxford University Press, 1990).

22. John N. Collins, *Deacons and the Church: Making Connections between Old and New* (Harrisburg, PA: Morehouse Publishing, 2002).

23. Collins, *Diakonia*, 230–31.

24. Frederick William Danker, ed., *A Greek-English Lexicon of the New Testament and Other Early Christian Literature* (BDAG), 3rd ed. (Chicago, IL: University of Chicago Press, 2000), 229–30.

25. Collins, *Deacons and the Church*, 58.

26. Bruce J. Malina and Richard L. Rohrbaugh, *Social-Science Commentary on the Synoptic Gospels*, 2nd ed. (Minneapolis, MN: Fortress Press, 2003), 193.

27. Bruce J. Malina, "Cup," in *Harper's Bible Commentary*, ed. Paul J. Achtemeier (San Francisco, CA: Harper and Row, 1985), 198.

28. Also John J. Pilch, *Stephen: Paul and the Hellenist Israelites*, Paul's Social Network: Brothers and Sisters in Faith (Collegeville, MN: Liturgical Press, 2008), 44–46.

29. John J. Pilch, *The Cultural Dictionary of the Bible* (Collegeville, MN: Liturgical Press, 1999), 135–40.

30. Collins, *Diakonia*, 194.

31. Ibid., 44–45.

32. Johannes P. Louw and Eugene A, Nida, eds., *Greek-English Lexicon of the New Testament*, 2nd ed., vol. 1 (New York: United Bible Societies, 1989), 364.

33. This is the topic of the first book in this series. See Bruce J. Malina, *Timothy: Paul's Closest Associate*, Paul's Social Network: Brothers and Sisters in Faith (Collegeville, MN: Liturgical Press, 2008).

34. Cited from Robert Charles Hill, trans., *Theodoret of Cyrus: Commentary on the Letters of Saint Paul*, vol. 1 (Brookline, MA: Holy Cross Orthodox Press, 2001), 135.

Chapter 4, pages 78–92

1. Kenneth E. Bailey, "Women in the New Testament: A Middle-Eastern Cultural View," *Theology Matters* 6 (2000): 3.

2. Joseph A. Fitzmyer, *Romans: A New Translation with Introduction and Commentary*, Anchor Bible 33 (New York: Doubleday, 1993), 731.

3. Ray R. Schulz, "A Case for 'President' Phoebe in Romans 16:2," *Lutheran Theological Journal* 24 (1990): 125–26.

4. Roger Gryson, *The Ministry of Women in the Early Church*, trans. Jean Laporte and Mary Louise Hall (Collegeville, MN: Liturgical Press, 1976), 3–4.

5. Sojung Yoon, "Phoebe, A Minister in the Early Christian Church," in *Distant Voices Drawing Near: Essays in Honor of Antoinette Clark Wire*, ed. Holly E. Hearon (Collegeville, MN: Liturgical Press, 2004), 30.

6. Elisabeth Schüssler Fiorenza, "Women in the Pre-Pauline and Pauline Churches," *Union Seminary Quarterly Review* 33 (1978): 158.

7. Esther Yue L. Ng, "Phoebe as Prostatis," *Trinity Journal* 25 (2004): 9–11.

8. E. A. Judge, "Cultural Conformity and Innovation in Paul," in *Social Distinctives of the Christians in the First Century*, ed. David M. Scholer (Peabody, MA: Hendrickson, 2008), 171.

9. Frederick William Danker, ed., *A Greek-English Lexicon of the New Testament and Other Early Christian Literature* (BDAG), 3rd ed. (Chicago, IL: University of Chicago Press, 2000), 885.

10. F. Blass and A. Debrunner, *A Greek Grammar of the New Testament and Other Early Christian Literature* (Chicago: University of Chicago Press, 1961), 5.

11. Ritva H. Williams, *Stewards, Prophets, Keepers of the Word: Leadership in the Early Church* (Peabody, MA: Hendrickson, 2006), 41.

12. Danker, *Greek-English Lexicon*, 870.

13. Bruce J. Malina and John J. Pilch, *Social-Science Commentary on the Letters of Paul* (Minneapolis, MN: Fortress Press, 2006), 53.

14. Robert Jewett, "Paul, Phoebe, and the Spanish Mission," in *The Social World of Formative Christianity and Judaism: Essays in Tribute to Howard Clark Kee*, eds. Jacob Neusner and others (Philadelphia, PA: Fortress Press, 1988), 149.

15. Gerd Theissen, "Social Stratification in the Corinthian Community," in *Christianity at Corinth: The Quest for the Pauline Church*, eds. Edward Adams and David G. Horrell (Louisville, KY: Westminster John Knox Press, 2004), 104–5.

16. Richard Saller, *Personal Patronage under the Early Empire* (Cambridge: Cambridge University Press, 1982), 1.

17. Malina and Pilch, *Letters of Paul*, 383.

18. Bruce J. Malina, "Grace/Favor," in *Handbook of Biblical Values*, eds. John J. Pilch and Bruce J. Malina (Peabody, MA: Hendrickson, 1998), 89–92.

19. David A. deSilva, *Honor, Patronage, Kinship and Purity: Unlocking New Testament Culture* (Downers Grove, IL: IVP Academic, 2000), 108, 111.

20. Bruce J. Malina and Richard L. Rohrbaugh, *Social-Science Commentary on the Synoptic Gospels*, 2nd ed. (Minneapolis, MN: Fortress Press, 2003), 406.

21. Danker, *Greek-English Lexicon*, 787.

22. Halvor Moxnes, "Patron-Client Relations and the New Community in Luke-Acts," in *The Social World of Luke-Acts: Models for Interpretation*, ed. Jerome H. Neyrey (Peabody, MA: Hendrickson, 1991), 248–49.

23. Stephen Charles Mott, "The Power of Giving and Receiving: Reciprocity in Hellenistic Benevolence," in *Current Issues in Biblical and Patristic Interpretation: Studies in Honor of Merrill C. Tenney*, ed. Gerald F. Hawthorne (Grand Rapids, MI: Eerdmans, 1975), 69.

24. Malina and Rohrbaugh, *Synoptic Gospels*, 252.

25. James D. G. Dunn, *Romans 9–16*, Word Biblical Commentary 38B (Nashville, TN: Thomas Nelson, 1988), 888; also Fitzmyer, *Romans*, 731.

26. Malina and Rohrbaugh, *Synoptic Gospels*, 370.

27. Kathleen E. Corley, *Private Women, Public Meals: Social Conflict in the Synoptic Tradition* (Peabody, MA: Hendrickson, 1993), 11–15.

28. Carolyn Osiek and Margaret Y. MacDonald, "Female Slaves: Twice Vulnerable," in *A Woman's Place: House Churches in Earliest Christianity* (Minneapolis, MN: Fortress Press, 2006), 97.

29. Corley, *Private Women*, 15–17.

30. Ekkehard W. Stegemann and Wolfgang Stegemann, *The Jesus Movement: A Social History of Its First Century*, trans. O. C. Dean (Minneapolis, MN: Fortress Press, 1999), 364.

31. James Malcolm Arlandson, *Women, Class, and Society in Early Christianity* (Peabody, MA: Hendrickson, 1997), 31–33.

32. R. A. Kearsley, "Women in Public Life in the Roman East: Iunia Theodora, Claudia Metrodora and Phoebe, Benefactress of Paul," *Tyndale Bulletin* 50 (1999): 209.

33. E. A. Judge, "St. Paul as a Radical Critic of Society," in *Social Distinctives of the Christians in the First Century*, ed. David M. Scholer (Peabody, MA: Hendrickson, 2008), 109–15.

34. Bruce W. Winter, *Roman Wives, Roman Widows: The Appearance of New Women and the Pauline Communities* (Grand Rapids, MI: Eerdmans, 2003), 21–22.

35. Ibid., 34–35.

36. Carolyn Osiek and David L. Balch, *Families in the New Testament World: Households and House Churches* (Louisville, KY: Westminster John Knox Press, 1997), 59.

37. Kearsley, "Women in Public Life," 192–93.

38. As is often the case, the words in the center of an inscription survive while the rest do not. As seen in this example, gaps are usually unavoidable.

39. Kearsley, "Women in Public Life," 207–8.

40. Carolyn Osiek and Margaret Y. MacDonald, "Dutiful and Less Than Dutiful Wives," in *A Woman's Place: House Churches in Earliest Christianity* (Minneapolis, MN: Fortress Press, 2006), 23–24.

41. Carolyn Osiek and Margaret Y. MacDonald, "Women Patrons in the Life of House Churches," in ibid., 210.

42. Moxnes, *Patron-Client Relations*, 264.

BIBLIOGRAPHY

Apuleius of Madauros. *The Isis Book: Metamorphoses, Book XI.* Edited and translated by J. Gwyn Griffiths. Leiden: E. J. Brill, 1975.

Arlandson, James Malcolm. *Women, Class, and Society in Early Christianity.* Peabody, MA: Hendrickson, 1997.

Babbitt, Frank Cole, trans. *Plutarch's Moralia.* Vol. 1. Loeb Classical Library. London: William Heinemann, 1927.

Bailey, Kenneth E. "Women in the New Testament: A Middle-Eastern Cultural View." *Theology Matters* 6 (2000): 1–11.

Barnett, James Monroe. *The Diaconate: A Full and Equal Order.* Valley Forge, PA: Trinity Press International, 1995.

Bartchy, S. Scott. "Undermining Ancient Patriarchy: The Apostle Paul's Vision of a Society of Siblings." *Biblical Theology Bulletin* 29 (1999): 68–78.

Bishops' Committee on the Diaconate of the NCCB and the Center for Applied Research in the Apostolate. "The Permanent Diaconate Today." Accessed at http://cara.georgetown.edu/pdfs/Permanent Diaconate.PDF.

Blass, F., and A. Debrunner. *A Greek Grammar of the New Testament and Other Early Christian Literature.* Chicago: University of Chicago Press, 1961.

Brandes, Stanley. "Reflection on Honor and Shame in the Mediterranean." In *Honor and Shame and the Unity of the Mediterranean,* edited by D. D. Gilmore, 121–34. Washington, DC: American Anthropological Association, 1987.

Collins, John N. *Diakonia: Re-interpreting the Ancient Sources.* New York: Oxford University Press, 1990.

———. *Deacons and the Church: Making Connections between Old and New.* Harrisburg, PA: Morehouse Publishing, 2002.

Committee on Diaconal Ministry. *History of Diaconal Ministry in the United Church of Canada*. Saturna Island, BC: Division of Ministry Personnel and Education, The United Church of Canada, 1991.

Connolly, R. Hugh. *Didascalia Apostolorum: The Syriac Version Translated and Accompanied by the Verona Latin Fragments*. Oxford: Clarendon Press, 1969.

Corley, Kathleen E. *Private Women, Public Meals: Social Conflict in the Synoptic Tradition*. Peabody, MA: Hendrickson, 1993.

Danker, Frederick William, ed. *A Greek-English Lexicon of the New Testament and other Early Christian Literature* (BDAG). 3rd ed. Chicago: University of Chicago Press, 2000.

deSilva, David A. *Honor, Patronage, Kinship and Purity: Unlocking New Testament Culture*. Downers Grove, IL: IVP Academic, 2000.

Du Boulay, Juliet. *Portrait of a Greek Mountain Village*. Oxford: Clarendon Press, 1974.

Duling, Dennis. "The Matthean Brotherhood and Marginal Scribal Leadership." In *Modelling Early Christianity: Social-Scientific Studies of the NewTtestament in Its Context*, edited by Philip F. Esler. New York: Routledge, 1995.

———. "Recruitment in the Jesus Movement in Social-Scientific Perspective." In *Social Scientific Models for Interpreting the Bible: Essays by the Context Group in Honor of Bruce J. Malina*, edited by John J. Pilch, 132–75. Leiden: E. J. Brill, 2001.

Dunn, James D. G. *Romans 9–16*. Word Biblical Commentary 38B. Nashville, TN: Thomas Nelson, 1988.

Eggan, Fred. "Kinship: Introduction." In *International Encyclopedia of the Social Sciences*, edited by David L. Sills. New York: Macmillan and the Free Press, 1968.

Elliott, John H. *What Is Social-Scientific Criticism?* Minneapolis, MN: Fortress Press, 1993.

Esler, Philip F. *Conflict and Identity in Romans: The Social Setting of Paul's Letter*. Minneapolis, MN: Fortress Press, 2003.

Fant, Clyde E., and Mitchell G. Reddish. *A Guide to Biblical Sites in Greece and Turkey*. New York: Oxford University Press, 2003.

Finucci, Valeria. *The Manly Masquerade: Masculinity, Paternity, and Castration in the Italian Renaissance*. Durham, NC: Duke University Press, 2003.

Fiorenza, Elisabeth Schüssler. "Women in the Pre-Pauline and Pauline Churches." *Union Seminary Quarterly Review* 33 (1978): 153–66.

―――. "The 'Quilting' of Women's History: Phoebe of Cenchreae." In *Embodied Love: Sensuality and Relationship as Feminist Values*, edited by Paula M. Cooey, Sharon A. Farmer, and Mary Ellen Ross, 35–49. San Francisco, CA: Harper and Row, 1983.

―――. "Missionaries, Apostles, Coworkers: Romans 16 and the Reconstruction of Women's Early Christian History." *Word and World* 6 (1986): 420–33.

Fitzmyer, Joseph A. *Romans: A New Translation with Introduction and Commentary*. Anchor Bible 33. New York: Doubleday, 1993.

Foley, Mary Ann. "Culture Area." In *Encyclopedia of Anthropology*, edited by David E. Hunter and Phillip Whitten, 104. New York: Harper and Row, 1976.

Gamble, H. *The Textual History of the Letter to the Romans*. Grand Rapids, MI: Eerdmans, 1977.

Garrison, Roman. "Phoebe, The Servant-Benefactor and Gospel Traditions." In *Text and Artifact in the Religions of Mediterranean Antiquity*, edited by Stephen G. Wilson and Michael Desjardins, 63–73. Studies in Christianity and Judaism 9. Waterloo: Wilfred Laurier Press, 2000.

Graves, Robert, trans. *The Transformation of Lucius Otherwise Known as The Golden Ass*. New York: Farrar, Straus, and Giroux, 1951.

Gryson, Roger. *The Ministry of Women in the Early Church*. Translated by Jean Laporte and Mary Louise Hall. Collegeville, MN: Liturgical Press, 1976.

Hanson, K. C., and Douglas E. Oakman. *Palestine in the Time of Jesus: Social Structures and Social Conflicts*. Minneapolis, MN: Fortress Press, 1998.

Hawthorne, John G. "Cenchreae: Port of Corinth." *Archaeology* 18 (1965): 191–200.

Hill, Robert Charles, trans. *Theodoret of Cyrus: Commentary on the Letters of Saint Paul*. Vol. 1. Brookline, MA: Holy Cross Orthodox Press, 2001.

Hohlfelder, Robert L. "Kenchreai on the Saronic Gulf: Aspects of its Imperial History." *The Classical Journal* 71 (1976): 217–26.

―――. *The Coins*. Vol. 3, Kenchreai: Eastern Port of Corinth. Leiden: E. J. Brill, 1978.

Horrell, David G. "From ἀδελφοί to οἶκος θεοῦ: Social Transformation in Pauline Christianity." *Journal of Biblical Literature* 120 (2001): 293–311.

Jewett, Robert. "Paul, Phoebe, and the Spanish Mission." In *The Social World of Formative Christianity and Judaism: Essays in Tribute to Howard Clark Kee*, edited by Jacob Neusner, 142–61. Philadelphia, PA: Fortress Press, 1988.

Judge, E. A. "St. Paul as a Radical Critic of Society." Chap. 4 (pp. 99–115) in *Social Distinctives of the Christians in the First Century*, edited by David M. Scholer. Peabody, MA: Hendrickson, 2008.

———. "Cultural Conformity and Innovation in Paul: Some Clues from Contemporary Documents." Chap. 7 (pp. 157–74) in *Social Distinctives of the Christians in the First Century*, edited by David M. Scholer. Peabody, MA: Hendrickson, 2008.

Karidoyanes FitzGerald, Kyraiaki. *Women Deacons in the Orthodox Church: Called to Holiness and Ministry*. Brookline, MA: Holy Cross Orthodox Press, 1998.

———. "Orthodox Women and Pastoral Practice: Observations and Concerns for the Church in America." *Saint Nina Quarterly* 3 (1999), http://www.stnina.org/journal/art/3.2.2.

Kearsley, R. A. "Women in Public Life in the Roman East: Iunia Theodora, Claudia Metrodora and Phoebe, Benefactress of Paul." *Tyndale Bulletin* 50 (1999): 189–211.

Kim, Chan-Hie. *Form and Structure of the Familiar Greek Letter of Recommendation*. Society of Biblical Literature Dissertation Series 4. Missoula, MT: Society of Biblical Literature, 1972.

Lampe, Peter. "The Roman Christians of Romans 16." In *The Romans Debate*, edited by Karl P. Donfried, 216–30. Rev. ed. Edinburgh: T&T Clark, 1991.

Liddell, Henry George, and Robert Scott. *Greek-English Lexicon with a Revised Supplement*. Oxford: Clarendon Press, 1996.

Louter, Becky Dodson. "Office of Deaconess and Home Missioner Program." In *Global Ministries: The United Methodist Church.* Accessed at http://new.gbgm-umc.org/about/us/mp/deaconess-homemissioner/.

Louw, Johannes P., and Eugene A. Nida. *Greek-English Lexicon of the New Testament*. 2nd ed. Vol. 1. New York: United Bible Societies, 1989.

Lutheran Deaconess Association. "What Is a Lutheran Deaconess?" Accessed at http://www.thelda.org/about/what_is.php.

Malina, Bruce J. "The Social Sciences and Biblical Interpretation." *Interpretation* 37 (1982): 229–42.

———. "Why Interpret the Bible with the Social Sciences?" *American Baptist Quarterly* 2 (1983): 119–33.

———. "Cup." In *Harper's Bible Commentary*, edited by Paul J. Achtemeier, 198. San Francisco, CA: Harper and Row, 1985.

———. "Grace/Favor." In *Handbook of Biblical Values*, edited by John J. Pilch and Bruce J. Malina, 89–92. Peabody, MA: Hendrickson, 1998.

———. "Hospitality." In *Handbook of Biblical Social Values*, edited by John J. Pilch and Bruce J. Malina, 115–18. Peabody, MA: Hendrickson, 1998.

———. "Love." In *Handbook of Biblical Social Values*, edited by John J. Pilch and Bruce J. Malina, 127–30. Peabody, MA: Hendrickson, 1998.

———. *The New Testament World: Insights from Cultural Anthropology.* 3rd ed. Louisville, KY: Westminster John Knox Press, 2001.

———. *Timothy: Paul's Closest Associate.* Paul's Social Network: Brothers and Sisters in Faith. Collegeville, MN: Liturgical Press. 2008.

Malina, Bruce J., and John J. Pilch. *Social-Science Commentary on the Letters of Paul.* Minneapolis, MN: Fortress Press, 2006.

Malina, Bruce J., and Richard L. Rohrbaugh. *Social-Science Commentary on the Synoptic Gospels.* 2nd ed. Minneapolis, MN: Fortress Press, 2003.

Miller, Charles H. "Corinth." In *Harper's Bible Commentary*, edited by Paul J. Achtemeier, 182–84. San Francisco, CA: Harper and Row, 1985.

Minear, Paul S. *The Obedience of Faith: The Purposes of Paul in the Epistle to the Romans.* London: SCM Press, 1971.

Mott, S. C. "The Power of Giving and Receiving: Reciprocity in Hellenistic Benevolence." In *Current Issues in Biblical and Patristic Interpretation: Studies in Honor of Merrill Tenney*, edited by Gerald F. Hawthorne, 60–72. Grand Rapids, MI: Eerdmans, 1975.

Moxnes, Halvor. "Patron-Client Relations and the New Community in Luke-Acts." In *The Social World of Luke-Acts: Models for Interpretation*, edited by Jerome H. Neyrey, 241–68. Peabody, MA: Hendrickson, 1991.

Murphy-O'Connor, Jerome. *St. Paul's Corinth: Texts and Archaeology.* Collegeville, MN: Liturgical Press, 2002.

———. *St. Paul's Ephesus: Texts and Archaeology.* Collegeville, MN: Liturgical Press, 2008.

Ng, Esther Yue L. "Phoebe as Prostatis." *Trinity Journal* 25 (2004): 3–13.

North American Association for the Diaconate. "Deacons in Anglican Churches." Accessed at http://www.diakonoi.org/naadinfo .html.

Olson, Jeannine E. *Deacons and Deaconesses Through the Centuries.* Rev. ed. St. Louis, MO: Concordia Publishing House, 2005.

Oporto, Santiago Guijarro. "Kingdom and Family in Conflict: A Contribution to the Study of the Historical Jesus." In *Social Scientific Models for Interpreting the Bible: Essays in Honor of Bruce J. Malina*, edited by John J. Pilch, 210–38. Leiden: E. J. Brill, 2001.

Origen. *Commentary on the Epistle to the Romans: Books 6–10.* Translated by Thomas Scheck. The Fathers of the Church: A New Translation. Vol. 104. Washington: Catholic University of America Press, 2002.

Osiek, Carolyn, and David L. Balch. *Families in the New Testament World: Households and House Churches.* Louisville, KY: Westminster John Knox Press, 1997.

Osiek, Carolyn, and Margaret Y. MacDonald. "Dutiful and Less Than Dutiful Wives." Chap. 2 (pp. 17–49) in *A Woman's Place: House Churches in Earliest Christianity.* Minneapolis, MN: Fortress Press, 2006.

———. "Female Slaves: Twice Vulnerable." Chap. 5 (pp. 95–117) in *A Woman's Place: House Churches in Earliest Christianity.* Minneapolis, MN: Fortress Press, 2006.

———. "Women Patrons in the Life of House Churches." Chap. 9 (pp. 194–219) in *A Woman's Place: House Churches in Earliest Christianity.* Minneapolis, MN: Fortress Press, 2006.

Patai, Raphael. *Family, Love and the Bible.* London: Macgibbon and Kee, 1960.

———. *Golden River to Golden Road: Society, Culture, and Change in the Middle East.* 3rd ed. Philadelphia: University of Pennsylvania Press, 1969.

———. *The Arab Mind.* Rev. ed. New York: Hatherleigh Press, 2002.

Pausanias. *Description of Greece.* Vol. 1. Translated by W. H. S. Jones. LCL. Cambridge, MA: Harvard University Press, 1978.

Pilch, John J. *The Cultural Dictionary of the Bible.* Collegeville, MN: Liturgical Press, 1999.

———. *Stephen: Paul and the Hellenist Israelites.* Paul's Social Network: Brothers and Sisters in Faith. Collegeville, MN: Liturgical Press, 2008.

Pitt-Rivers, Julian A. "Honour and Social Status." In *Honour and Shame: The Values of Mediterranean Society*, edited by J.G. Péristiany, 19–77. Chicago: University of Chicago Press, 1966.

———. "Kinship: Pseudo-Kinship." In vol. 8 of *International Encyclopedia of the Social Sciences*, edited by David L. Sills, 408–13. 18 vols. New York: Macmillan and the Free Press, 1968.

———. *The Fate of Shechem or the Politics of Sex: Essays in the Anthropology of the Mediterranean*. Cambridge Studies in Social and Cultural Anthropology Series 19, edited by Jack Goody. Cambridge: Cambridge University Press, 1977.

Rassam, Amal. "Women and Domestic Power in Morocco." *International Journal of Middle Eastern Studies* 12 (1980): 171–79.

Rhoads, David. "Performance Criticism: An Emerging Methodology in Second Testament Studies—Part I." *Biblical Theology Bulletin* 36 (2006): 118–33.

Rohrbaugh, Richard L. "Introduction." In *The Social Sciences and New Testament Interpretation*, edited by Richard L. Rohrbaugh, 1–15. Peabody, MA: Hendrickson, 1996.

Rothaus, Richard M. *Corinth: The First City of Greece: An Urban History of Late Antique Cult and Religion*. Leiden: E. J. Brill, 2000.

Saller, Richard. *Personal Patronage under the Early Empire*. Cambridge: Cambridge University Press, 1982.

Salmon, J. B. *Wealthy Corinth: A History of the City to 338 BC*. Oxford: Clarendon Press, 1984.

Schaff, Philip, ed. *A Select Library of the Post-Nicene Fathers of the Christian Church*. Vol. 11. New York: Christian Literature Company, 1889.

Schulz, Ray R. "A Case for 'President' Phoebe in Romans 16:2." *Lutheran Theological Journal* 24 (1990): 124–27.

Scranton, Robert, Joseph W. Shaw, and Leila Ibrahim. *Topography and Architecture*. Vol. 1, *Kenchreai: Eastern Port of Corinth*. Leiden: E. J. Brill, 1978.

Stegemann, Ekkehard W., and Wolfgang Stegemann. *The Jesus Movement: A Social History of Its First Century*. Translated by O. C. Dean. Minneapolis, MN: Fortress Press, 1999.

Stern, Wilma Olch, and Danae Hadjilazaro Thimme. *Ivory, Bone, and Related Wood Finds*. Vol. 6, *Kenchreai: Eastern Port of Corinth*. Leiden: E. J. Brill, 2007.

Strabo. *Geography*. Vol. 4. Translated by Horace Leonard Jones. LCL. Cambridge, MA: Harvard University Press, 1988.

Theissen, Gerd. *The Social Setting of Pauline Christianity*. 2 vols. Philadelphia, PA: Fortress Press, 1982.

———. "Social Stratification in the Corinthian Community." In *Christianity at Corinth: The Quest for the Pauline Church*, edited by Edward Adams and David G. Horrell, 97–105. Louisville, KY: Westminster John Knox Press, 2004.

Thucydides. *History of the Peloponnesian War: Books III and IV*. Translated by Charles Forster Smith. Cambridge, MA: Harvard University Press, 1975.

United Church of Canada, "Discernment of Ministry: Diaconal Ministry." Accessed at http://www.united-church.ca/adultlearning/preparing/discernment/diaconal.

Walters, James. "Phoebe and Junia(s)—Rom. 16:1-2, 7." In *Essays on Women in Earliest Christianity*. Vol. 1, edited by Carroll D. Osburn, 167–90. Joplin, MO: College Press, 1995.

Werner, Walter. "The Largest Ship Trackway in Ancient Times: The Diolkos of the Isthmus of Corinth, Greece, and Early Attempts to Build a Canal." *The International Journal of Nautical Archaeology* 26 (1977): 98–119.

Williams, Ritva H. *Stewards, Prophets, Keepers of the Word: Leadership in the Early Church*. Peabody, MA: Hendrickson, 2006.

Winter, Bruce W. *Roman Wives, Roman Widows: The Appearance of New Women and the Pauline Communities*. Grand Rapids, MI: Eerdmans, 2003.

Wiseman, James. *The Land of the Ancient Corinthians*. Studies in Mediterranean Archaeology. Vol. 50. Göteborg: Paul Aström, 1978.

Yoon, Sojung. "Phoebe, A Minister in the Early Christian Church." In *Distant Voices Drawing Near: Essays in Honor of Antoinette Clark Wire*, edited by Holly E. Hearon, 19–31. Collegeville, MN: Liturgical Press, 2004.

Young, Margaret. "On the Go with Phoebe Snow: Origins of an Advertising Icon." *Advertising and Society Review* 7 (2006): 1–31.

SCRIPTURE
AND ANCIENT AUTHORS INDEX

Canonical Documents

Genesis

13:8	26
18:4-5	62
18:8	62
18:10	63
19:1-2	62
19:12-13	63
20:1-18	24
20:11	24
20:12	24
37:4-5	25
37:9-14	25
37:16	25
37:26-27	25

Exodus

2:11	26
21:15	26
21:17	26

Leviticus

20:9	26
23:3	29
25:35-39	26

Numbers

6:1-21	95

Deuteronomy

15:7	26
15:9	26
15:11-12	26
22:1-4	26

2 Samuel

3:3	25
11:3	8
12:24	8

1 Kings

1:10	25
1:11	8
1:15-16	8
1:28	8
1:31	8
2:7	25
2:13	8
2:15	25
2:18-19	8
2:21-22	25

Jeremiah

17:21-22	29

Sirach

3:1-11	26
20:14-15	84

Ancient Writings and Inscriptions

INDEX OF PERSONS AND SUBJECTS